WE DON'T RECOVER, WE GET BETTER

TONY DONACHY

Published in 2024 by Toast and Beans Books

Copyright © 2024

Tony Donachy has asserted his right to be identified as the author of this Work in accordance with the Copyright, Designs and Patents Act 1988

ISBN Paperback: 978-1-3999764-7-3
Ebook: 978-1-3999822-4-5

All rights reserved. No part of this publication may be reproduced, stored in a retrieval system, or transmitted in any form or by any means, electronic, mechanical, photocopying, recording or otherwise, without the prior permission of the copyright owner.

A CIP catalogue copy of this book can be found in the British Library.

Cover photography by Helen Baillie

Published with the help of Indie Authors World
www.indieauthorsworld.com

To Caitlyn and Siana, the girls who saved my life

ACKNOWLEDGEMENTS

Thank you to the following people who have helped me with this book and much more:

Helen Donachy, Caitlyn Donachy, Siana Donachy, Paul Donachy, Peter Donachy, Geoff Dearie, Neil Mc Auley, Katey Murray, Linda Thompson, Mariem Omari, Scott Kyle, John, Piddy, and Helen Baillie.

NATURE OR NURTURE

Most of society seems to be going through some kind of great awakening. We appear to be living in a time where people are starting to question themselves and their existence in greater numbers and on a deeper level than they ever have before. It's as if, after so many centuries of ambling in apathy, more and more of us are begging to question: *Who am I?* Or more specifically: *Why am I the way I am?* And that's a question that I – on some levels willingly, and on others not so willingly – have asked myself more than once. Some of us have less choice about searching our souls than others.

For some of us it feels as though life has backed us into a corner, and we've been left to search the depths of our psyche for a lost sense of meaning or purpose. The trouble is, once you've opened the door to self-exploration it never really shuts. There's a reason why the wise men and mystics call it a journey, as one question usually seems to be answered by another.

It's during that newfound quest for a deeper level of self-understanding that we begin to ponder what could be one of life's oldest and most important questions: Is it nature or nurture?

Are we born who we are, or do our experiences mould us into what we become?

THE FIRST ANSWER

When I first got clean, the answer was simple. I was born with the disease of addiction. Yet while the answer was simple, the explanation was anything but. And when I asked at the fellowship meetings, the best anyone could come up with was: 'It must have been God's will.' So, I was fucked from the start.

Did God see some unknown potential in me that he forgot to tell me about, then decide to deal me a shit hand for the entertainment of seeing how I handled things and played the game?

But against all odds, I have turned out rather well. So maybe I played better than expected.

This is the typical addict mindset, though. We live in a constant state of ambivalence where we feel both worthless and self-important at the same time. No matter what, it's all about us. But most of us feel like that for a reason. I've not met one person with addiction issues that wasn't emotionally hypersensitive; we seem to feel things more deeply than others. So, when negativity is projected our way, it wounds us. And because, in most cases, our experiences have taught us that sharing our feelings with others can be dangerous, we keep those feelings to ourselves. Yet this just adds to our sense of exclusion and the idea that no-one else could possibly understand how we feel.

We're incredibly complex creatures. So complex in fact that most of us have no idea who we are or where we are supposed to fit into this world.

That is how it felt for me, and although I would never presume to speak for anyone else, it does seem to be a common theme.

I'm afraid all I can offer to any of you is an honest account of my own experiences and how it felt to be me, in the hope that others might find it helpful or at the very least entertaining enough to keep reading. But I have been clean for over nine years now, and I like to think I've learned something along the way.

The truth is that for most of my life I felt like an outsider, like an alien child that had been left stranded on a strange planet, patiently waiting for the mother ship to come back and collect me. Or, at some points, like a monster being chased by angry villagers with pitchforks and burning torches.

I couldn't assimilate; society didn't understand me, and I didn't understand society.

I know this may sound more like the start of a horror or science fiction novel than a book about addiction, but these feelings aren't uncommon. I've heard hundreds of addicts tell their own stories over the years, so I know there are lots of others who grew up feeling just like me.

And I suppose it's our lack of identity and self-understanding that leads us to cling to all the labels that society gives us. Addict, alcoholic, I have a disease.

Imagine you spent your whole life trying to figure out just what the fuck was actually wrong with you, who you were, where you belonged, or why you felt so broken. Then when you were at your most vulnerable, the most lost and broken you had ever been, someone came along and said that they didn't just know what was wrong with you, but they had a name for it and knew how to fix it. They offered you that sense of identity you had been searching for all your life. They said they knew where you belonged in the world and knew exactly how you felt. You would grasp it with both hands and defend it, even with its flaws. Well, that's what I did… at least in the beginning.

Ok, so the whole fellowship ideology doesn't really make sense to me anymore, but there was a time when it did. And I'll never forget how I felt after my first meeting.

I felt safe, accepted, and enthusiastic, all at the same time. Full of what people call the 'fellowship fire'. You get all charged up and want to rush out into the world like an evangelist so you can tell everyone how good the meetings are and that every addict can be saved. That God and the higher power can change their lives if they are just willing to ask for help.

I must have been the most annoying person on the planet. But I was just so grateful not to be using drugs anymore.

Don't worry, I'm not one of those people that gets clean and condemns drug use. Far from it. I used drugs because I liked them – I'll expand on that later – and I had some good times using them. And if I could use drugs without them destroying my life, and the lives of everyone around me, I'd probably still be doing it. But my using took me to a pretty dark place, and I have no desire to ever go back there again. So, any future recreational drug use would take a lot of careful consideration.

To be honest, I'm perfectly happy without them. Well, as perfectly happy as a person can be.

And when I say drugs, I also mean alcohol, by the way. There are no degrees of separation here. A substance is substance, as far as I'm concerned, regardless of how socially acceptable it might be.

We can talk about how heroin and crack cocaine destroy lives, which they do, there's no doubt about that. But in my experience, which I can assure you is more than most, alcohol is arguably the most destructive drug on the planet. And that's mostly because of how socially acceptable and easily accessible it is.

Back to the point: that overwhelming sense of gratitude was the driving force behind my journey to getting clean. And even though I no longer agree with that kind of ideology, it was a massive part of my journey. So, no matter how some of this might sound, I'm very grateful for what meetings and fellowships did for me.

DEMONS AND THE END OF THE WORLD

Despite an odd start in life as an overweight, socially awkward child that spent most of his time being bullied, I eventually evolved into a relatively average scheme boy. Even if it did take a while to get there.

Again, the real problem was that I didn't seem to fit in anywhere. I always felt out of place, no matter what group I tried to attach myself to. Over the years I was a goth, a punk, an emo – before emos were even a thing – before becoming a ned (non-educated delinquent) and car thief who carried knives and fought with other neds over patches of spare ground that no-one else wanted.

The only consistent theme was drugs, which seemed to be the foundation of all of my relationships, no matter what circles I moved in. I bought them, I used them, I sold them; they were always there.

People say that the first step to getting better is admitting that you have a problem, but that's not quite true. Yes, it's true that you can't address something if you can't bring yourself to admit that it exists. But the real first step is actually doing something about it. And it took a long time for me to go from acceptance to actively changing.

I openly admitted that I had a problem; I was even proud of it at one point. It became my way of defining who I was before I knew who I was. The thought of life without drugs was an alien concept to me.

I suppose somewhere some part of me secretly wanted to stop, but if it was there, it was well hidden.

As you can imagine, there were various points when my using did make me very unhappy. It wasn't like I hadn't tried to stop. I had, more than once, but I just never managed to. I could barely get through a day without something in my system. Up until I got clean, the longest I had ever stopped for was about three months. And that was back in 2001 when I stopped using heroin. At that time, I was as determined as I had ever been, but life was unbearable.

As we are now starting to learn, drugs aren't really the problem. And when you take them away, you're left with all the reasons that led you to use them in the first place. And I just wasn't ready to look at those back then.

From 2001 I never did use heroin again, which I suppose is something. I even convinced myself I was clean at one point because I wasn't sticking needles in myself anymore. However, the truth was that I was anything but clean. I would take anything else that was going, and in copious amounts, too.

I even believed I had a spiritual experience after buzzing furniture polish once. Who knows, maybe I did. If I've learned anything, it's that the energies of the universe truly do work in mysterious ways. Funnily enough, that's what I was convinced I was just about to figure out – the secrets of the universe and all its mysteries. But just as I was about to be given all the answers, I woke up, and I never managed to get back to whatever realm I had visited.

Now that should give you a fair idea of how serious my addiction was. It gave me a fair idea, too. My using didn't just take me to some dark places, but some terrifying places… and some happy places, too. It was never enough to stop me, though. I was as messy on the inside as my life was on the outside.

From the second I woke up until the moment I fell asleep my head was full of broken bottles, a battleground. That was if I even managed to sleep at all, which was an ever-increasing rarity. As was anything solid passing my lips. I was always starving but had no appetite. It was as if my stomach had forgotten how to process food.

When I finally got clean, I hadn't slept in twelve days and hadn't eaten for nine. I know that because I was counting. I always counted how many days I could go without sleep or sustenance, and I found it miraculous the things the human body can endure and still keep running. Not literally, of course; I couldn't run the length of myself back then.

I didn't eat for another two days after I got clean either, and even then all I could manage was half a sandwich my niece had left on the kitchen counter. All I could think about was how I was even alive.

As if surviving without food or sleep doesn't sound bad enough, on the rare occasions when I did manage to shut down, I woke up to the unknown terror that I now know was sleep paralysis. And that really is fucking terrifying, by the way, for anyone who hasn't had the privilege of experiencing it. I would wake up in the small hours of the morning feeling as if I was being pinned to the mattress by some unearthly creature, unable to move anything but my eyes, which would flick around the room in darkness.

Now that I'm relatively sane, and capable of rationalising my thoughts – at least for the most part – I know that sleep paralysis is just my brain waking up before my body. In my less rational days, though, I was more than capable of convincing myself that I had my own personal demon sent to torment me. It was as if I was supposed to be kept awake at night so I could torment myself about all the terrible and selfish things I had done in my life, both real and those perceived by my own inappropriate guilt. I was even convinced I could hear the demon breathing. Once I thought I actually saw it sitting in the corner of the room staring at me. Of course, it wasn't. It was the furry hood of my parka hanging over the weights bench.

I wasn't sure if psychosis affected my sleep or if my lack of sleep made the psychosis worse, but either way they fed into each other quite nicely.

Some people say that cannabis is harmless, but I'm not so sure. I'm not saying it's dangerous either, just that not everyone has a mind that's suited to using it. I think THC (tetrahydrocannabinol) has the ability to soothe a mind that's already calm or make a chaotic mind all the more chaotic; it all depends on the person. My mind certainly wasn't suited to it, and it made me extremely paranoid.

Funny thing is, I knew it wasn't good for me, just like I knew I had a drug problem. But I smoked weed for most of my life, regardless of whether it was good for me or not, from the age of 14 right the way through until I finally stopped using drugs at 34.

Smoking weed gave me a funny way of making sense of things. I thought my paranoia helped me to see the world for what it was. And I was obsessed with conspiracy theories – freemasonry, the Illuminati, and the occult. Because I couldn't sleep, I stayed up all night doing what I called 'research', hunched over a laptop, switching between YouTube videos of Bohemian Grove and lizard people. Or watching documentaries about Heinrich Himmler and the Nazi Thule Society, and Anton Lavey and the Church of Satan, mixed with horror movies and X hamster. As you can tell, I wasn't a very well man.

It got to the stage where I would look up city maps, scanning them for street patterns laid out in the shape of owls or pentagrams, or any other occult symbology. I'm not saying that satanists or lizard people run the world, and I'm not saying they don't; this is not that kind of book. All I am saying is that if they do, there's not very much we can do about it. And looking into it obsessively the way I did dramatically affects your ability to function in society.

Using Tony didn't care about that, though. He was prepared for the end of the world and slept with a loaded crossbow beside the bed and a hunting knife under his pillow.

As wild, and indeed dangerous, as I know this all sounds, it all ties in with that feeling of impending doom. And that is another thing you hear us addicts speaking about quite a lot. It was just as real as my sleep paralysis demon, which is very real when you're living in that experience.

That impending doom was a feeling that had been with me since I was a child. It's hard to describe, but it was as if some unknown threat was coming for me, waiting for me at every corner. I never knew its name or what it was. All I knew was that it was dark and harmful, and for some reason it wanted me.

Years later, my sponsor and I would laugh about lots of things that I would never have found funny until I spoke about them and had the chance to process them properly. One of those was the fact that I was a 34-year-old man who lived with his mum and couldn't be trusted to use the washing machine, but who was ready to take on the end of the world with a crossbow and a hunting knife.

My poor wee mum is the one I really feel sorry for in all this. She was the only person that would listen to me. Not because she wanted to, but because we lived in the same house, so she had no escape. Trapped, listening to the rantings of her lunatic son 'educating' her while he drank whisky and smoked grass that made her feel sick. Abusing her prescription. Ironically, I now rely on that same medication for similar conditions. I have scoliosis and permanent spine injury, just some of the many conditions I've been diagnosed with since I got clean – some of which are hereditary. Turns out using drugs hides more than your feelings.

I've not just had to learn how to manage multiple medications safely, but I also now understand how much my mum needed those tablets.

There are a lot of people in 'recovery' that would never use dihydrocodeine or any other type of opiate-based medication. Some would even count it as a relapse, but I strongly disagree. To me, being able to use this kind of prescription medication safely, after abusing it for as long as I did, can only be seen as a clear sign that people can change.

And it's not like they just put you on this medication. I had to have some very long and honest conversations with my GP. My prescriptions were strictly monitored, and if there had been any cause for concern, I knew they would immediately start looking for alternatives.

I think the big difference between me and some other people is that I don't see addiction as a disease. Although there may be underlying contributing factors, I personally think the whole disease ideology is a bit of a cop-out. When we're using, we do selfish things for reasons we don't fully understand and can't fully explain. Things that leave us feeling guilty and shameful. Having a disease that we're powerless over kind of sugarcoats that a little, making our guilt easier to swallow. There's a big difference between explanation and justification.

Since I got clean, my goal has been to try and figure out why I made the choices I made, not to justify them. Because, like it or not, they were choices. One of my choices was abusing my mum's prescription so badly that she went without her medication because she didn't feel comfortable keeping it in the house.

Towards the end, I was taking so much codeine that I was having a non-fatal overdose almost every day. My eyes were rolling into the back of my skull while I was being enveloped by the mattress, then from nowhere I'd sit bolt upright with a jolt, as if at a subconscious level my body was saying, 'Not today, Tony.'

THE BUILD-UP

Strangely, to anyone looking in from the outside, my life finally seemed to be ok. In fact, I appeared to be doing better than I ever had. Ok, I was 34 and still living with my mum. But after years of instability, it looked like I had finally pulled my shit together enough to do something with my life.

I had made it through college and was studying journalism and creative writing at the University of Strathclyde. And that was quite an achievement for someone who grew up with dyslexia before the education system recognised dyslexia as the learning disability that it is.

I wasn't really prepared for that type of lifestyle, though. Most people plan to go to university, whereas I had kind of got there by accident.

I was what demographers would describe as long-term unemployable. I had never managed to hold a job down for longer than a few months, if I got one at all. Most of the time I didn't even bother to look for work as I didn't see the point. However, we know that the government doesn't like that very much, so the Department for Work and Pensions (DWP) assigned me to something called the work programme. This is where they force you to look for work, and if you don't, they stop your benefits. It wasn't an idle threat either; they meant it, as I soon found out.

It wasn't as if I didn't want to work or have a stable life. I just wasn't stable enough. Forget about a job, I couldn't even manage the Jobcentre appointments that were supposed to help me find one. So, the inevitable happened and they stopped my money.

I went to the doctor and openly spoke about my issues with a medical professional. Not just about my drug use, but my mental health including thoughts of violence and the impending doom of the apocalypse. She gave me an Alcoholics Anonymous leaflet and told me to go for a walk round the park, but I had spent a lot of time walking around parks and my mental health had never got any better.

I had no money, no job, and no support – except for my poor wee mum, of course. There was only one thing for it, I was going to have to go to college. I knew lots of people that had been to college, and while I might have been off my nut, I was still smarter than most of them. How hard could it be? And they would give me a bursary which would get the DWP off my back. And who knew, my mum might have eventually been proud of me.

But when I applied for my course, I got rejected. I had to write a handwritten essay on my choice of five subjects. I chose the conflict in the Middle East, certain that I had done enough 'internet research' to write five-hundred words on that. When they saw the childlike hieroglyphic scrawling of a grown man who had stopped attending school at the age of fourteen, and practically hadn't written anything since, they said I wasn't suitable and doubted I could handle the course work.

I suppose I couldn't really blame them; I might as well have written the essay in crayon. But being told I wasn't suitable made me more determined. So determined that I barged into the office of some guy – whose name I will never remember – steaming drunk, with my hand in a plaster cast because I had broken it punching a wall during a temper tantrum, and with a half-bottle of vodka hanging out of my back pocket. Shouting about dyslexia, which wasn't officially diagnosed till I was at uni, I accused them of discrimination.

I got to re-sit the entry assessment, this time with a laptop, and I passed. One blurry year and a toxic relationship later, I was at university.

I wasn't emotionally ready for that shit; it was beyond me. It was just like being back at school with that alienating feeling of not fitting in. I wasn't sure how to dress, never mind how to act. That isn't surprising given the fact that I had always felt out of place in the world, but there was more to it than that.

As I'm sitting here writing this, I've realised there is an important part of the story, so let's dial back before I keep going forward.

Before I started college, I wasn't just an unemployable drug addict. I had pretty much become a full-scale hermit following an incident at an afternoon drinking session at a neighbour's house. Unbeknown to me, one of the guys I was sitting with had a younger brother who happened to have a grievance with my young brother, which meant the other guy had a grievance with me. I know it sounds like something from the playground, but that's just how things are in a housing scheme. People get trapped in a time warp, and some never make it to adulthood, no matter how old they are.

Anyway, I digress. There we were, all friendly, then as I reached down to pick up my can of Stella, something hit me on the head. I looked up to see that this guy had hit me over the head with an ashtray, and he had no intention of stopping. All I could do was cover up as best I could to try to protect my face. Eleven times he hit me; I know, because I counted the lumps.

He left me with eleven lumps, two cuts, and a small skull fracture where the corner of the metal ashtray caught me. I can still feel the dent.

As soon as he stopped swinging, I grabbed him and dragged him out into the hallway, with the intention of having a few swings of my own. Before I knew it, there were three people dragging me off him. And that's when I knew it was a set-up. I also knew that there were sharp knives in the kitchen, and if I didn't leave while I still could, the situation might get a lot worse. After that, I hardly ever left the house; and if I did, it was never without a weapon.

To go from that kind of mentality to being at university, without any real support, was just overwhelming.

I was in my thirties and still had no clue who I was. I turned up on my first day dressed like a pound-shop Danny Dyer. A month later I was dressed like a lecturer. I even got myself one of those leather satchels they were all carrying. I think the contents of mine might have been a little different, though. Well, maybe they also had the half bottle of brandy (I was quite surprised to find out just how many university lecturers were functioning alcoholics. You can always spot one of your own.), but I doubt they had a bag of street valium in their satchel. In saying that, you never know.

The case for my glasses was full of joints, and I still had a barber's razor in my pocket… just in case. If you asked me in case of what, I still couldn't tell you. I just felt it was better to have and not need it, than need and not have it. I had no boundaries back then, either – well, fewer boundaries.

I had a lecturer called Dr Higgins who we used to call Higgy. I would shout at him from the other end of the corridor 'Haw Higgy', as if we were friends working on a building site. He would just give me a mortified wave and keep walking in the other direction.

But for the headcase that I was, I had some big plans.

When I first got clean, people used to tell me to stick with it and I'd get a life beyond my wildest dreams. And I would say, 'I don't know about that, mate. My dreams are pretty fucking wild!' I wasn't lying either. My dreams were big.

Fuelled by drugs, long-term psychosis, and YouTube research, my dream was to become Glasgow's answer to Hunter S. Thomson – an investigative journalist who flew around the world, high on copious amounts of high-quality substances, while I gained intelligence on the Satan-worshipping cannibalistic lizard people that secretly governed our society. It's a far stretch from a grown man that probably couldn't function without his mum, but you can't fault my creativity.

After being clean for a while – and I do mean a while – I finally figured out what those people meant when they said a life beyond your wildest dreams.

They meant a life where we feel comfortable in the world, in our lives, even in our own skin. A life of contentment and self-acceptance, and the feeling that we belong, without being haunted by those feelings of sickening discomfort and inexplicable fear we had all known so well and lived with for so long.

And I suppose a life of happiness and contentment does seem fantastical for someone who had spent their whole life believing happiness was attainable for everyone else but not for them. Someone who had convinced themselves that the problem must lie with the other people, inventing reasons to justify that belief. Reasons like: these other people couldn't see the world for what it was; they hadn't faced the same challenges I had; they didn't have my parents; or whatever other shit we make up about people without really knowing who they are or where they've been.

LONELINESS AND ISOLATION

Even though I was surrounded by people, I was incredibly lonely. So lonely that I would sleep with any woman who'd let me, whether I was attracted to them or not. It wasn't about the sex. All that mattered was that for a brief moment I felt connected to someone, even if I knew deep down that the connection wasn't real.

Addicts don't just use drugs; they also use people, because they seek the comfort they struggle to find within themselves. It doesn't matter if it's heroin, cocaine, sexual partners, or social media. It's all about some form of comfort, connection, or acceptance. For instance, people who use cocaine do it because it gives them what feels like a superhuman feeling of self-confidence. They feel energised, more comfortable in social situations, find it easier to talk to potential partners, and it enhances their sexual performance. It provides them with that thing they felt they were missing. And it's the same with heroin; it just offers a different type of comfort.

But as for sexual partners, my self-esteem was so low that it didn't matter who they were or if I found them attractive. What mattered was that they found *me* attractive. I felt appreciated, accepted, even loved in some way. It didn't even matter if had to pay them. All that mattered was that they were there.

Towards the end of my using, my body was so run down that I wasn't even capable of having sex most of the time. All I really wanted was company and someone to listen to me and my self-indulgent warbling about how I was one of life's victims. What I failed to realise was that the person listening to me was having a worse time of it than I was; most likely worse than I could probably imagine.

Being one of life's victims – a claim most of us could make in one way or another – didn't stop me from victimising others. I robbed or manipulated money from anywhere and anyone, including family and friends. I'd dip their pockets, even steal their jewellery if they left me alone long in their houses long enough. I even managed to manipulate the neighbours into giving me money for prescription medication.

MONEY

Although I was only pulling in around twelve hundred pounds a month, I wasn't used to having such a stable income at the time, and I didn't know what to do with it. Well, actually I did know: spend it. They say that, as with so many other things in life, it's all about attitude, and a poor person will end up poor no matter how much money you give them because that is how they see themselves. And that, at least in my case, made perfect sense.

After my dad died and we sold his house, I walked away with thirty thousand pounds. I'd never seen so much money, but it didn't do me much good as it was spent within a year. I did try to do something sensible with it and started a landscaping business. But it landed on its arse within the first three months, due to my insatiable need for cocaine and prostitutes.

And it was the same with my student loan and the money I got from the university's disabilities department. At the beginning of my first – and only – year at university, I finally got an assessment from an educational psychologist, confirming that I was not only dyslexic but had the worst case of dyslexia the woman had ever seen. This meant that I was entitled to a two-thousand-pounds loan from the disabilities department of The University of Strathclyde… which I did eventually pay back, albeit at the lowest possible rate.

I was supposed to use the money to buy a laptop, printer, and software to help with my coursework. Instead, I went on the Christmas bender that would tear my family apart, before eventually bringing us back together.

While I was out doing all the things a lot of men claim to enjoy, but most of them secretly don't, my family was bearing the brunt of my emotional issues. In return, they got to watch me slowly destroy myself.

Whether we want to admit it or not, addicts will always look for new ways to justify or excuse their behaviour and how it affects the people around them. I blamed everybody except me. It was my mum's fault, my dad's fault, the people who bullied me at school's fault – though that did play a big part in it. It was society's fault, even God's fault. My dad and all my uncles were alcoholics, and I knew that some sort of genetic pre-disposition might be a thing, so in my mind I couldn't help it even if I wanted to. That is another reason the disease ideology doesn't sit well with me. It feeds into the justification mindset of the old me, and I'm trying to get as far away from that guy as I can.

Then the day came when my excuses weren't enough any longer. These were the excuses of a child… and I was grown man. I realised that regardless of what had happened in my life, my choices were my own. But even though that was something I was consciously aware of, I still couldn't stop myself. I wasn't sure if I was too far gone to ever get my life together. I wanted to; I just didn't know how.

THE FESTIVE SEASON

All this carnage in my life took place at the end of the year. We were in the run-up to Christmas when my mum made it clear that my brother was coming over with his kids.

My brother and I hadn't really spoken in months. Not just because I was someone no-one wanted to be around, but because he had spent eighteen months battling his own demons and was finally doing well. He had been doing voluntary work with addicts in the east end of Glasgow for a year or so, which probably made me even more difficult to tolerate. Every day he could see people slowly pulling their lives back together, and there I was not even trying.

Alcohol usually brought out the worst in me. It always has. So my poor wee mum, who in her own way facilitated, enabled, and accommodated my using throughout my whole life, begged me not to drink.

It would not have been the first festive season I had ruined. One of the memories that haunts me the most is something that happened back in 2001, the same year I came off heroin. I'm saying memories, but the truth is that I can't remember anything about it, so my memory of it has been created from the first-hand accounts of other people.

I blacked out at a house party on New Year's Eve and woke up the next day covered in blood. Luckily, it was mine. I still can't remember anything that happened that night, which I'm still glad about, to be honest. But apparently, I got a bit too rowdy and offended a few people and got myself a sore face. Nothing unusual there; it was Glasgow, after all.

However, that's not the part that bothers me. It's what I was told happened after it that still keeps me awake at night sometimes. It seems I went home and got a knife, with the intention of going back to the party. And when my mum and my brother stopped me, I was so angry that I chased my brother round the house with the eight-inch knife. He had to eventually lock himself in the bathroom, with me stabbing holes in the door like Michael Myres.

My brother and I were always fighting; we were best friends that hated each other. The truth is that in all the time that's passed, we've never spoken about that incident. And any time I have brought it up, my brother says he can't remember it. That's the funny thing about trauma. Sometimes it saves you from itself. But whether he remembers it or not, there's no way something like that didn't affect our relationship.

I was no stranger to what kind of monsters were lying dormant inside me, but even that wasn't enough to stop me. I handled guilt like any other emotion and just pushed it as far down as it would go, clouding it over with drug use.

Despite all that and knowing what the possible outcome might be, I wasn't happy about my mum asking me not to drink that Christmas, and with my spiteful addict logic I decided to buy fifty Valium instead. To me that sounded like a fair compromise. I would still get to avoid reality but wouldn't be drunk, so technically my mum would get what she had asked for.

In the spirit of Blackadder's Baldrick, I had a cunning plan. I'd take half the tablets on Christmas Eve and the other half on Christmas Day. That would have been bad enough, but that's not how things went. Me being me, I took the whole bag on Christmas Eve and ended up in such a state that my then 64-year-old mother had to scrape her adult son off the floor and put him to his bed.

This was after he had bounced off every wall in the house and pissed on his PlayStation because he couldn't find the toilet.

That was it: game over, the final straw. She was done, and rightly so. No-one should have to put up with that.

I'm still actually surprised it took her so long to get to that point. Watching someone you love slowly destroying themselves while they take their behaviour out on you must be one of the worst forms of suffering. But having to turn your back on them to protect your own mental and emotional health must be heartbreaking.

If you do ever find yourself in that situation, please try not to feel bad about it. Supporting an addict is hard work, especially when they're so lost in their addiction that they aren't even willing to help themselves.

Finding myself homeless – not for the first time – I managed to get myself a one-bedroom flat. In fairness, I had been looking for one for a while, because I think we had all seen this situation coming.

But I'll never forget what she said to me before I left. 'You can go and drink and take drugs till oblivion, but I won't watch you kill yourself any longer.'

I remember being so angry with her. That wasn't anything unusual; I was angry all the time. But I remember wondering how she could do this to me, her son. In my head, the way I had turned out was at least partly her fault, and now she was turning her back on me. Obviously now I can see how ridiculously selfish it was to even think that after everything she had put up with. But at the time I just felt abandoned, and I honestly thought I would never forgive her for it.

Suddenly, for the first time ever, I was alone. And I don't mean the I-feel-so-isolated-because-no-one-understands-me alone. This was the I-had-no-one-else-left-in-the-world kind of alone.

After two days of living in my new flat, I looked around my dark living room with the black bags still covering the windows and thought, *Fuck it*. I had been thinking about committing suicide for longer than I can remember, and now I felt it was time. I had it all planned out. I was going to slit my wrists, then put on a pair of rubber Marigolds with another pair of gloves over the top so that no-one would see the blood. Then I'd walk to the hospital with the bottle of vodka I was already drinking.

My reasoning was simple. If I made it to the hospital before I bled to death, my life had some kind of purpose and was meant to continue. If not, I would bleed to death in the street, and the world would be a better place for it.

Even in my darkest moments I was indecisive. The truth was I didn't know what I wanted. All I knew was that I wanted my pain, and the pain I had caused everyone else, to stop.

Just as the knife was hovering over my wrist, something happened.

I can't speak for anyone else that's ever planned or attempted to take their own life. But for me, in that moment, all the different people and the life events I associated with them started flashing though my mind. My mum, my brother, even my dad. None of them, I'm sorry to say, gave me any reason to change my mind. Then the faces of two little people appeared in my mind. They were my brother's two oldest kids – he has four now, but they were the only two he had at the time.

All I could think about was how much those kids loved me. And for the first time ever, I felt like I just might not be the worthless piece of shit I had always believed I was.

Even now I don't fully understand what happened. It wasn't as if this was new information or something I didn't already know. What I do know is that was the most important thought I've ever had in my life.

Two things never happened that night: I never killed myself, and I never finished that bottle of vodka. And in the years that have followed, I have never opened another bottle.

ASKING FOR HELP

As I said, I openly knew I had a problem, but I just didn't know how to fix it. Let's face it, if you're in a public toilet with a shoelace round your ankle, using dirty needles to inject heroin into your feet, you know you have a problem.

One of my favourite songs was 'I Am An Alcoholic' by rock band NOFX. It's not uncommon for one problem to lead to another and in my case, my substance use became my identity. Using drugs wasn't just something I did; it became who I was.

We all have a breaking point, though, and that night of loneliness was mine. It was my Ground Zero, my rock bottom moment.

I had decided that wasn't going to be my last night, but beyond that I had no idea what to do. I just put my coat on and left the flat. I wasn't even sure where I was going, I just knew that it had to be somewhere other than where I was. I got to the payphone round the corner and tried to call a taxi to the only other place I could go. Yup, you guessed it, back to my mum's. I knew I wasn't welcome, but there really was nowhere else for me to go.

The payphone swallowed my money. Then, as if things couldn't get any worse, all those opiate-based painkillers decided that it was time to leave my system at the same time. And I'm afraid to say that I got so stressed out that I lost control of my bowels and I shit myself in the street.

I know this all sounds a bit grim, but I promise the uplifting part is on its way. And the whole point of this book is to show people where drugs took me to, without omitting any of it, even the worst parts. No matter how embarrassing.

I want to tell you how I managed to grow from that person to the person I am today. If I left out the worst parts, I'd only be lying to myself while doing all of you a disservice.

I obviously had to go back to the flat and clean myself up before I went anywhere, which also meant facing the bottle of vodka. But through sheer determination I managed to leave it alone.

After that, I walked for an hour and a half in the pissing rain, crying like a child just to get to my mum's, even though it was highly possible that I'd be turned away at her door. As much as Mum had enabled my using over the years, she's far from the softest or most sympathetic of creatures. She is a wee Glesga maw, after all.

When she opened the door and saw the state of me, I think she knew things were serious and she let me in – which is something I'll always be grateful for.

And there I was, after just a couple of days of living on my own, back at my poor wee mum's house, crying and telling her I didn't want to live anymore. As much as she undoubtedly wanted to help me, she couldn't, as she had no idea what I was going through. So, she suggested that I phone the only person we knew who possibly could – my brother. And that was an even more daunting prospect than going to my mum's in the first place.

As you can probably guess, I was more than a little reluctant. I was pretty sure he wouldn't help me if I asked, and I felt vulnerable enough without being rejected. But I was so desperate that I had no other choice. I don't know why, but when he answered the phone, everything just started pouring out, like a dam bursting. All those years of pain, and shame, and guilt. I don't think I even stopped for a breath.

And he understood. I couldn't believe it. For the first time in my life, I had opened the gates to the swampland of my emotions, and someone wasn't just listening... they understood me.

We had lived in the same house for most of our lives, used drugs together, fought, fallen out, and argued, as I suppose all brothers do. But this was the first time we had ever been truly honest with each other.

I was crying, he was crying, our mum was crying. We were just all so overwhelmed.

TRYING TO ACCESS SUPPORT

Finally, I was through the door. By taking that first step, I had gone from acknowledging that I had a problem to actively doing something about it, which was a big thing. But what came next was even bigger.

Going through that, and my family being forced to witness what came over the days that followed, is one of the main reasons I've managed to stay clean all this time. Because, and I'm sure I speak for all of us when I say, none of us would ever want to go through that again. Despite what certain people and ideologies might say, we are not all the same. Our addictions and stories might be similar, but every addict is different. Our drug use affects us all in different ways. And getting clean is different for everyone, too.

For some, the meetings and the programmes are enough. Others need counselling, or even to be completely removed from society to stand a chance of getting clean. Then there are the ones that don't need to get clean at all. They just need to work on what's called harm reduction to reduce their using and form a healthier relationship with substances.

However, there is one certainty. If an addict does want to get clean, they're going to have to go through some form of detox. Sorry, folks, but there really is no avoiding it.

The question I was asked most when I started sharing my stories on social media about addiction and getting clean was: How do I get clean? It sounds like the answer would be obvious: Stop using. But it is an understandable question, because for a lot of people – including myself at one point – the idea of getting clean sounds like trying to make the impossible possible.

I always tell everyone the same thing. No matter what their drug of choice is, or if they want to go to rehab, they get clean by doing meetings. Always start with harm reduction, gradually reducing your drug use over a set period of time, at a pace that suits you. Trying to come off everything at once is like an overweight person trying a diet that restricts them to a thousand calories of raw carrots a day. It's both unrealistic and unsustainable. And a hard detox, going straight cold turkey, isn't just difficult. It's dangerous, and I would strongly advise against it.

This part of my story is going to sound a bit hypocritical, I'm afraid, because I did exactly what I've just told you not to do. And as hypocritical as it might be, at least you know that I'm speaking from experience.

Doing a hard detox wasn't my intention. I did try to access support and seek advice, but apparently there was no help available. I was told I'd have to wait two weeks before I could even speak to a doctor, and I was advised to keep using until I could be seen.

I tried to get a place in a community rehab, but they told me there was a three-month waiting list just for a referral. And what was their advice? Yup, you guessed it: keep using.

Well, I'm sorry, but I didn't have three months, or two weeks. My detox had started.

A fortnight later, when I finally did get to see a doctor, she informed me that detoxing the way I had done was a really stupid thing to do, especially with the alcohol. Giving up alcohol can cause something called delirium tremens, also known as the DTs, which can cause seizures so severe that the body can shut down completely.

After the doctor had finished giving me her opinion, she did something which I think was equally as stupid as my detox, and also very unexpected. She tried to put me on a methadone prescription. A methadone script when I was already two weeks' clean? That made no sense to me at all. And she wasn't the only one.

Three months later, while I was doing voluntary work, I was advised to register with the local community addiction team so that I could be allocated an addiction worker to support me with the benefits system or housing applications if I needed it. I didn't personally think I needed a worker, but again it was better to have and not need than need and not have. However, the addiction worker tried to put me on a fucking meth script, too.

In my opinion, methadone isn't like other medications. In fact, when it comes to addiction, I don't think methadone should be classed as a medication at all. It's more like a behaviour stabiliser. Something that helps people move away from that negative cycle of using, scoring, and committing criminal acts, while they establish a support network and engage with relevant services. Then when they're ready, it should be gradually reduced until they're in the right place for full detox. Calling it medication just feeds into the disease ideology, which I really don't feel is helpful.

But I was already three months' clean and doing voluntary work, so I was about as stable as a 'recovering addict' gets. The guy was quite pushy about it, too, and he sounded more like a salesman than an addiction worker. In the end, I had to be very direct and just tell him that if he gave me a script, I would just throw it way.

At the time I couldn't figure out why they were so keen, but years later I found out that there's a lot of money in methadone.

YOU'VE GOT TO GET CLEAN FOR YOURSELF

I'm lucky enough to be able to say that I've survived more than one detox in my life. And in my experience, I found that coming off prescription painkillers and alcohol, along with everything else I was taking, was far worse than coming off heroin. And I'm not in any way saying giving up heroin is easy.

I was twenty and had been living in a squat – not for the first time. This particular shooting gallery was in a block of high-rise flats in Grange Park which is, or at least was, the only housing scheme in Blackpool at the time. Not that the rest of Blackpool was too glamorous either.

I had been in this squat for about four months, and it was just as you would imagine. Damp running down the walls, brown mattresses on the floor, and dirty needles in every corner. It sounds horrendous, and it was, but I had never been so grateful just to have a roof over my head and somewhere warm and dry to sleep after many months on the street.

But, as most addicts do, I ended up owing someone. I had a wild weekend in someone's flat, injecting ecstasy and amphetamine, and apparently ran up quite a bill – one that I had no intention of paying. This resulted in the guy I owed the money to – a very calm and reasonable man – threatening to set me on fire and take my shoes if I didn't have his money the next time he saw me. Though why anyone would want a homeless person's shoes is beyond me.

To anyone who has never been in the environment of a using heroin addict, this probably all sounds a bit ridiculous. But the next time you're at the bus stop and you happen to hear two opiate enthusiasts arguing, don't put your earphones in and try to blank them out. If you actually listen to what's being said, you'll realise that your ridiculous is someone else's way of life.

I had seen this man attack someone else with a hoover, over a jar of pickled cabbage, so I wasn't going to hang about to find out if he was serious with his threats.

Unlike some of the unfortunates you might find living in a situation like that, I had a family – well, a mum – who had been asking me to come home for a while. I told you she was an enabler, although she never knew about my heroin use at the time.

After two years of hostels, squats, and sleeping rough, I decided it was time to go back to Glasgow and face the ghosts that were waiting for me there, so that I didn't have to face the speed freak fire where I already was. But this left me with a dilemma. I loved my mum, but I thought she was better off without me, which is partly why I had stayed away for so long. But I also loved heroin. So, being the king of compromise that I was, I came up with another cunning plan. Using heroin would be ok as long as I was only smoking it and not using needles. At least then I could hide my use and I wouldn't be covered in track marks. And there was no chance of my mum finding me with a needle hanging out of me.

Over the course of a few weeks hiding in the squat, I weaned myself off injecting and got back onto running lines on the foil. I was so serious about it that I wouldn't even let anyone inject themselves in front of me. And I managed to cut myself down from four bags a day to just one, which was an impressive feat in itself.

The day I finally got the bus home, I took half a bag with me that was already on the foil, with the intention of scoring when I was back in Glasgow. And that wouldn't have been a problem... until I saw my mum, and everything changed. Seeing how she took me in and forgave me after all the things I had done in the past, I realised I couldn't put her through any more.

I couldn't put her through me using heroin and all the trouble it might cause; she'd put up with enough. So, I took my foil, rolled it up into a ball, and threw it away. And I've never touched heroin since.

I admit I felt like shit for a few days and, as I said, I just replaced the heroin with alcohol and weed, which to me was clean back then.

The big problem was that I did the physical detox – the heroin was out of my system – but I avoided the emotional work that goes along with it. And more importantly, I didn't do it for me. I didn't give up heroin because I wanted to. I gave it up for someone and how my using would affect them. And as noble as that might sound, getting clean for other people doesn't work long term. It can be a good starting point, but living without drugs is a trade-off.

At some point you have to make the decision over whether your life is genuinely better with drugs or without them. Secretly, I missed heroin, and giving it up was a sacrifice I wasn't really willing to make – at least, not at that time. Making such a sacrifice resulted in me resenting my mum and the rest of my family for forcing me to make a decision that they didn't even know I had made. And in the meantime, I took every other drug available, trying to fill the void that heroin left.

COCKROACHES AND FLIES

When I was finally ready to get clean, it was worse than anything else I had ever experienced in my life. My using had nearly killed me more than once, but coming off all those substances at the same time was nothing short of harrowing. I was trembling from my marrow to the surface of my skin. Twitching, convulsing, suffering cramps and muscle spasms. I couldn't hold my jaw steady, and my teeth were chattering like a battery-operated ventriloquist's dummy. One minute I was burning up, the next minute I was freezing, as if I was a lizard who couldn't find the right spot to bask in the sun.

The doctor asked if I'd had any hallucinations during my detox, and in particular if I had seen any spiders, which is apparently quite common. I said I hadn't seen any spiders, but I did see other things… and felt them, too. It felt like I had invisible things crawling on me, causing an itch that wouldn't stop no matter how hard I scratched.

I could see flies in my peripheral vision that almost seemed to be taunting me then vanished when I looked at them. There were cockroaches scuttling across the floor. But the strangest thing was that at one point I looked at a towel hanging over a radiator, and I swear the fibres were moving like grass in the wind. And all I could do was lie there in my delirium and let it all happen.

I got through it, though. But being tormented by crawling skin and spectral insects was just the beginning. As unsettling as all this sounds, what was going on inside me was just as bad. I had never felt so hollow. It was as if someone had reached in and pulled my heart out and just left an empty space, a vacuum where any part that allowed me to feel remotely human used to be.

It wasn't a new feeling; I had always felt hollow, using drugs to fill the void. Now there was nothing to fill the space, and I was finally finding out just how deep it was. And just like the flies and the towel fibres, I just had to sit with it and hope that it would finally stop.

Unfortunately, that's the part people struggle with most – the inside stuff. Horrible though it is, the physical stuff is over in a few days. But those feelings, those emotions, feel like they're going to be part of you forever.

Trust me, though, they won't. It does get better, but you just have to do the work and give it time.

MY FIRST MEETING

Unbeknown to me, although I was still going through the physical part of my detox, my real work was about to begin. This wasn't a time for messing about. I'd said I wanted to change, and there were people in my life that were just as determined about my change as I was and who were going to make sure I stuck to it. After a long night of sweating and shivering on my mum's couch, my brother appeared like some 'recovery avenger' ready to drag me off to my first fellowship meeting.

Before I go on to talk about meetings and 12-Step programmes, because I know there are some sensitive wee snowflakes out there, I'm not out to offend anyone or belittle their journey.

I'm neither promoting fellowships or saying that they have no place in the world. Nor am I suggesting that one fellowship is better than another, or that my way of thinking makes more sense than anyone else's. I'm merely speaking from my own experience and telling you about the things that I did, what I learned, and what makes sense to me. By all means, you should try things for yourself and come to your own conclusions about what works and makes sense and what doesn't. What worked for me might not work for you, and vice versa. Horses for courses and all that.

So there I was, a hollowed-out human, lying shaking and sweating on my mum's couch. And suddenly my brother appears in front of me like some 'let's-get-clean recovery avenger'. I'm sure he had his boxers on over his trousers, but what do I know? I was still delirious.

Another thing you should know is that I'm only using the word 'recovery' because that's the accepted term. Personally, I don't think it makes much sense, but I'll explain why later. There's no point in jumping about and going off on tangents any more than I already am.

I was dragged off the couch, and we were on our way. Then things got even worse than I had been expecting. We didn't just have to go outside; the idea of that was bad enough. But no, I also had to face public transport, and not just one, but two buses. Two buses is not something you want to face on the second morning of your detox, when the whole world feels like one big, never-ending bad trip, and all you want is to be swallowed up by the ground beneath you.

I felt so exposed, as if the whole world could look into my soul and see every shameful, embarrassing, and selfish thing I had ever done.

And it gets worse. We met people my brother knew, and they would not stop trying to talk to me. I mean, they were very nice people. They kept trying to reassure me that they had been where I was and knew how it felt, and that if I stuck with it things would get easier. One of them actually ended up becoming my sponsor. But at the time all I could think was, *Please, fuck off and leave me alone.*

Years later, my sponsor and I spoke about the first day we met, and I apologised for being an ignorant, anti-social zombie, and compared myself to something from the walking dead. But he said he just remembered me looking sad.

Funny thing is, in the beginning I thought sadness was what I was signing up for. I knew drugs had taken me to a dark and depressing place, but I couldn't imagine a life worth living without them.

Most of us have preconceived ideas about fellowship meetings, as we've all seen them in some film or TV series. I imagined dimly-lit rooms filled with people sitting in a circle holding hands and talking about God while they felt sorry for themselves, foaming at the mouth, fantasising about crack pipes. (By the way, that is surprisingly one of the few drugs I've never tried. I had seen enough people crawling on the floor smoking bits of carpet fluff to know that it wasn't for me, and downers were always more my thing.) Or people with guitars, singing verses of 'Kumbaya'.

But that could not have been further from the truth. Apart from the sitting in a circle with candles and holding hands, because that part is true. Well, sometimes.

Instead, I found myself in a room full of guys who looked like extras from *The Football Factory*. There was nothing weak or apologetic about these guys; not in the slightest. These were men that knew themselves and were trying to make peace with some of the things that they had done in their lives. And to tell you the truth, I felt more than a little intimidated. It was worse than being on the bus.

At first, I thought about just getting up and leaving. And if my brother hadn't been with me, I probably would have. I'm glad I didn't, though. Instead, I managed to push through all that fear and anxiety and had what turned out to be an uplifting and life-changing experience.

Fellowship meetings are a lot more formal and organised than you would expect them to be, too. They're very structured and even have a format and a chairperson, who in this case just happened to be my future sponsor.

They also have tea and biscuits, not that I could stomach them. It was another two days before I could manage solids. But there were certainly no guitars or any hymn singing of any kind.

The most common format for meetings is a share, which is where someone is invited to speak about their own personal experience.

Then you take a wee break for the aforementioned tea and biscuits. Afterwards, the meeting is opened up to the rest of the room, and everyone else is allowed to speak. This gives people the chance to say how they identified with the person sharing, and to talk about their own experiences or the things they're experiencing at their own stage in the journey.

After that conversation with my brother, I had already experienced how powerful sharing and identifying with someone else could be. But when that guy started speaking, I wasn't sure how to feel. It was pretty much a running commentary of my own life. Not just the drugs, or the behaviours, the stolen cars, the violence, the lies, or the theft and manipulation. Or the part where my family had to turn their back on me because they couldn't bear to watch me destroy myself any longer -- all of which I could relate to.

But in an indirect way, this guy was describing everything in my life that I felt guilty or ashamed about. And that's what really got me. He wasn't just describing things I had done; he was telling me I how I felt. Things I had never told anyone and that I felt stupid for even thinking. But it was as if he was inside my head.

In the second half of the meeting, I found words coming out of my mouth without me even thinking about it. I still don't know why; it was as if the words were being drawn out of me, like I was sitting in the audience at a Derren Brown show. Obviously, it had all been just sitting there under the surface waiting to come out.

I'd had no intention of saying any of it out loud, and especially not to a room full of intimidating strangers. Yet there I was telling them all about how worthless and alone I felt. I didn't let it all out, of course; there was a lot that remained hidden until I finally started the programme. And even then, I never spoke about everything at meetings.

The truth is that meetings aren't really a safe space, so don't share more than you have to. Yes, they emphasise the importance of personal anonymity, and they remind everyone that what you hear at the meeting stays at the meeting. But at the end of the day, people gossip and talk about each other. It's part of who we are.

Some advice I received, and always tried to stick to, is 'Don't say anything at a meeting you don't want other people to repeat', because there's a good chance some of them probably will. Some things are only for yourself, your sponsor, and your closest circle of friends.

THE POWER OF COLLECTIVE CONSCIOUSNESS

Although some of you might not be familiar with the set-up or format of fellowships, you probably know they are synonymous with the idea of some type of higher power. That understandably confuses some people, because they think that God and higher power are the same thing. They're not. God is God in whatever way God makes sense to you, whereas a higher power is anything that has more power than you at any given moment. It could be your mum, your kids, the drugs you're craving and finally got to use... and yes, even God, if that's your thing. It could even be something as simple as having someone to talk things through with. The higher power is all-inclusive, it includes acts of God. But then again, your mum, kids, or indeed drugs could be seen as a form of God's real-world intervention, all depending on your perspective. Again, it's whatever works for you.

Anyone who has been to a meeting will also tell you that there's a strange, indescribable, uplifting energy in the room. Some of the less sceptical have no hesitation to say that it's the presence of God. As a non-believer, that was a concept I easily dismissed. But I couldn't – no-one could – deny that the energy was there. It was tangible, you could feel it, and if it wasn't God, what was it?

Unknowingly, this was my first experience with collective consciousness.

We all emit energy. Some call it an aura, the more scientific among us might say EMF (electromagnetic frequency), and the late great James Brown simply called it a vibe. How you choose to describe it isn't important; it's all the same thing. All that does matter is that it's very real, and it's something we've all felt in one form or another.

Have you ever walked into a room and for no reason felt either comfortable or uncomfortable? Or maybe you've shaken someone's hand for the first time ever and just decided, 'Yup, they're one of mine, that's one of my humans.' Or, 'Nope, they're not for me.' That's the kind of energy I'm talking about. An invisible but ever-present energy flowing through everything that most of us will never fully understand.

Every single cell in the human body can produce up to 0.7 millivolts of electricity, and we have 35 billion cells. That's 2.65 trillion volts of electrical current, and that's just one body. These are all approximations, of course; there's new research being done all the time, so no doubt by the time you read this, the figures will be different. But I encourage you to look into the subject for yourselves because it really is fascinating.

All that energy doesn't stay contained within us; it radiates out. Imagine that kind of energy filling a room, carrying with it all the emotions and intentions of the people it radiated from. If those emotions and intentions were positive and continuously poured out into the same place over and over again, would it not be possible for those people to create a healing space without even realising it? And this isn't just happening at fellowship meetings. It's happening in churches, chapels, mosques, synagogues, and temples of all kinds.

And it isn't just constrained to places of recognised religious or spiritual significance either. It's happening at yoga studios, raves, concerts, music festivals. Anywhere that people gather with a unified intention or shared emotional attachment to the same belief ideology. And the more we gather in those places, the more energy they absorb, and eventually they become places of power. They hold all that energy, which is continuously being charged with the emotional intent of everyone that visits them.

Now imagine yourself sitting in that space feeling broken and unlovable, surrounded by the people that helped to create it, all sharing the same beliefs and adding to the energy that's already stored there. And they don't just welcome you in; they ask you to be part of it.

Would that be enough to make you question your own beliefs about God and spirituality?

THINGS NO-ONE EVER SPEAKS ABOUT

To anyone who has never been through it, the process of getting clean might seem like a simple one. You stop using, you figure out why you were using, and you do your best not to do it again. And while that might be the essence of it, it isn't quite as simple as that. There are a lot of things that I know most, if not all, addicts go through when they get clean, but no-one ever seems to talk about.

No doubt you're wondering how I know every addict goes through these things. Simple, I spoke about them openly with other people, and they all knew exactly what I was talking about.

One of the first things I experienced when I first got clean was what I can only describe as a period of extreme emotional turbulence. I was all over the place. I couldn't figure out what I was feeling or why. There were times when I even found myself walking along the street laughing and crying at the same time. People must have thought I was out on day release, but inside it felt like I was being pulled apart.

For over two decades I had been numbing myself from every aspect of myself and my life that I didn't want to face. But now the gates were open, and emotionally I was child again. I was seven years old, trying to process and understand a lifetime of trauma, substance abuse, and poor life choices.

Ok, so I wasn't using drugs when I was seven, but that was when my addictive behaviours started.

Drug addiction gets all the focus, simply because it's the most dramatic and it seems to have the worst impact on people lives. But that's only due to the stigma surrounding it and the impact it has on the people offering support, or even society in general. But there are other ways addiction can affect people which are arguably more difficult to manage. Food addiction, for example, is something that millions of people struggle with on a daily basis. 2.8 million people die every year due to obesity and other related conditions every year, yet it still doesn't command the same attention as something like heroin. But to the person struggling with it, the thoughts and emotions are exactly the same. The only things that differ are the 'drugs of choice', the external behaviours. And it's those external behaviours that seem to determine how seriously we view the severity of the addiction, not how that addict feels within themselves.

Back in those early days of being clean, I remember thinking that I would never get through this, that it was too difficult. I thought about using every day. And there were only two things that got me through it – determination and honesty.

I had made a commitment, not only to myself but to the people who cared about me the most, that I would see this through. And I wasn't willing to let any of us down.

I didn't have the ability to be completely honest with my family... at least, not back then. But that was probably a good thing, because it would just have given them even more to worry about. However, I checked in with my sponsor every day, and I spoke as honestly as I could at meetings while still trying to keep myself safe. To be honest, I didn't seem to have much choice. There were nights when my mouth just opened and the things that were ready to come out came out, leaving me wondering, *Why the fuck did I just say that?*

Something else I found was that as my mind began to wrap itself around the idea of life without drugs, I felt and sometimes was even compelled to act on the urge to revert to other styles of addiction and other negative coping strategies.

Looking back, food was actually my first addiction, simply because as a child it had the ability to change how I felt. So, I know first-hand how serious it can be. I used to hide in the bathroom with the door locked and eat biscuits, and quickly found out that KitKat wrappers don't flush. By the time I was ten years old, I weighed ten-and-a-half stone.

But as we know, enough is never enough, and before long I was looking for new ways to get my dopamine fix. The next big thing for me was porn. I started using pornography when I was nine, after being introduced to it by an older friend. I wasn't being groomed or anything untoward. He just shared something he'd discovered with a friend who so happened to be a couple of years younger than him.

I started off with magazines, as I think most people do. But I wasn't just looking at the images, I was obsessed with them. I would hide them in my room and get them out whenever I had a spare moment alone. Then one day I found something that blew my little ten-year-old porn-obsessed mind.

Like most people, I was a curious child and would wander about the house exploring drawers and cupboards when my parents – still together at the time – weren't home.

On one occasion, I ventured into the fitted wardrobe in my mum and dad's bedroom and found a load of VHS tapes on the bottom shelf. They were stacked three-high, the full length of the double wardrobe.

Looking back now, I understand that when it comes to addiction my dad's issues were very similar to mine. And that has helped me re-process and make peace with a lot of things from my childhood. And those similar issues more than likely meant similar interests.

I was ten years old, had just discovered my dad's secret porn library, and I watched them all. It got to the stage where I would tell my mum I was sick so I could stay off school and watch things children should never see. I was watching women have sex with dogs and horses! A child's mind isn't ready to process something like that, and I certainly wasn't mentally or emotionally equipped for it. And it completely warped my view of sex as I was going through puberty – something I had work through later when I was going through the Steps and the counselling that followed.

The next one is a little different as it's something that's not usually associated with addiction, but it will make sense when I explain it.

I developed all these addictive behaviours as a coping strategy because I was being bullied at school. That wasn't the only unpleasantness I've experienced in my life, just the unpleasantness that was happening at the time. But in the long run, my coping strategies only made things worse. I was getting bullied for being overweight, but I ate to help me cope, then put on more weight which meant the bullying got worse. Then I started watching porn to distract me from my unhappiness, and that led to me being even weirder and more socially awkward than I already was. And the longer the bullying went on, the angrier I became.

When it comes to anger, there are generally two types of people.

There's the explicitly angry person, the kind that spews their anger out into the world. Like weekend hooligans, or the woman who abuses the supermarket cashier because they've run out of carrier bags. Then there's the implicit ones, who internalise things and hold onto them, in most cases even silently blaming themselves for things that are totally outwith their control.

I have been both the explicit and the implicit angry person at different stages of my life. But as a child, all of my anger was internalised until it became overwhelming, and I had to find a way of releasing it.

The first time I cut myself, I was twelve. I was in my granny's bathroom, and I cut myself across the wrist with a disposable razor. I'm still not sure why I did it or what was going through my mind at the time. Since then, I've convinced myself that I was just curious to see what it would look like. But the truth is that I was looking for some kind of release, and I found it.

I cut myself regularly for years, throughout most of my teens. Sometimes I managed to keep it hidden, but it was very impulsive, so a lot of the time the marks were clearly visible.

My mum and my brother used to come in when I was sleeping and check me for fresh cuts, which I know must have been traumatising for them. But just like everything else I've done, I can't take it back; all I can do is try to balance it out as best I can. And as upsetting as it may have been for them, they were only spectators. I was the one going through it.

I know self-harm isn't really thought of as a form of addiction, but for me it falls into a similar category in the sense that it was another obsessive-compulsive behaviour I used to change the way I felt and help me manage my emotions.

In the early days when the drugs weren't there to help me handle stressful events and emotional obstacles, I didn't revert to cutting myself, but I definitely did think about it.

For the first few weeks of my recovery, I was living between my mum's house and my own flat, simply because we all agreed that living on my own would be too much too soon, and my family wanted to keep a close eye on me. Every day for about a week I would walk past the phone box at the end of the street, and there would be a long, rusty screw lying on the ground. Every time I saw it, I had the same intrusive thought: *Pick that up and ram it into your face*. Obviously I didn't, but porn and food were a regular if not daily indulgence in the early days of getting clean. And especially when I was going through the programme and the counselling work that followed.

If you're in the same situation, when you decide to put the drugs down you might find yourself being tempted to revert to other old coping strategies. If you do, don't worry about it, it's just part of the process. Just make sure you're sharing your thoughts with the appropriate people, and you'll be fine.

Something else you're going to have to get used to is that you're going to see drugs and alcohol everywhere you go. I would walk down streets I had walked down a hundred times and see pubs and off-licences that I could swear were never there before. It was like an unwelcome superpower. I could smell people smoking grass from a bus stop half a street away. I would walk into the toilets in McDonald's and smell heroin or see rolled-up train tickets which people had used to sniff lines off the cistern. It didn't matter where I went, drugs just seemed to be everywhere.

Dealers, too. Ones I knew, ones I didn't know, people offering me drugs, selling drugs, dropping bags of smack into the cups of people begging in the street. I started to think that maybe the God of the meetings was real and was testing me in some way. But the real reason is far more interesting and easier to explain.

Our brain is a very clever thing. It's the original supercomputer. Every day it processes information in ways we can't imagine. But what's even more interesting is that we are computer programmers, and most of us have no idea how the computer works or even what it's capable of.

Our internal computer is capable of processing 11 million bits per second, whereas the conscious mind can only process around 50; not 50 percent, just 50 bits. If we were consciously aware of all the information that surrounded us, we'd probably explode.

Our brains only show us what it believes we'll find to be the most relevant information, based on our interests and emotional responses.

Have you ever been on Facebook and coincidentally seen adverts for the things you've just looked at on Amazon? I like to call it 'information by association', and it's happening in your brain all the time.

This selective awareness to things we seem most interested in is caused by our RAS, or Reticular Activating System. In the most basic terms, it's the RAS's job to show us what it thinks we want or desire most. Well, when you're an addict, drugs aren't just wanted or desired; they are the centre of your universe. So, it's only natural that your brain would go looking for them if they're not there.

This next one's a bit weird, but trust me it does happen. You might go through a phase of thinking that everyone fancies you. I know it sounds a bit silly, but it is a thing, and like every other thing it happens for a reason.

Imagine that you've spent your whole life feeling worthless, shunned, isolated, misunderstood, and feeling like you have no real place in the world. Then people suddenly start treating you as if you matter, as if you're finally worth something… and you don't have to do anything. They don't want anything from you. They don't want money, they're not trying to sell you drugs, they don't seem to want anything in return. That would take a bit of getting used to, right?

While that's happening, something else is happening, too. How you feel about yourself is beginning to change. You don't realise it, but you've started to make the shift from being worthless to being worth something.

You've not had the chance to do any real work on yourself, and you've not developed any real self-worth, but you now realise that you're worth more than you ever thought. You're starting to look and feel better, and most likely smell better. Your nervous system isn't being suppressed and confused by whatever chemicals you were filling your body with, meaning the old libido is back with a vengeance. And on top of all that, people are treating you like an actual human, which can only mean one thing to someone who hasn't had the chance to develop any real emotional awareness: they obviously want to sleep with you.

In some cases, you might be right. Some of them might want to sleep with you, which can lead to its own problems. But most of them don't. Most of them are only showing you kindness because they either understand what you're going through, or they can just see how broken and vulnerable you are. They're proud of you for trying, and they feel that you need more love and less judgment.

FINDING A SPONSOR

Filled with the healing holy spirit of N.A. (Narcotics Anonymous), I was completely sold on the fellowship doctrine. And I was sure that I finally knew what had been wrong with me my whole life: I had a disease. The disease of addiction, which was something I found very comforting at the time. What was even more comforting was that it was a disease I could eventually recover from, if I was just willing to put the work in.

I put aside other commitments and followed everything to the letter. I went to meetings every day. I did the thirty meetings for thirty days, then ninety for ninety, as was advised.

When I was about a month-and-a-half clean, I decided to find myself a sponsor and start the programme. There are different versions of the programme and, as I said already, I'm not here to promote that any fellowships are better than another, or that one version of the programme is better than others.

I'll be talking about the N.A. 12-Steps working guide, simply because it's the one I worked with. The 12-Steps guide was originally created by the founders of Alcoholics Anonymous, Bill Wilson and Dr Bob Smith in 1935, then adapted as other fellowships began to emerge while still promoting the original disease ideology. After having conversations with people from other fellowships, the N.A. 12-Steps working guide seems to be the most in-depth version of the programme, and the one that most people seem to want to avoid. It certainly takes longer to work through than the others and is a big commitment. It took me eighteen months in total.

My sponsor and I agreed to one step per month but, as you would expect, there were obstacles along the way, and some steps were more challenging than others.

A lot of people at the meetings will ask you if you've found a sponsor and started the steps, and it can almost feel as though they're trying to pressure you into it. Don't let them. They're just telling you what other people told them, and most of those people have never done it themselves. Most of the people telling me to go through the programme had never made it past Step Three, and pretty soon you'll find out why.

Taking this on before you're ready can sometimes do more harm than good. The programme opens doors, not just to the past but to who you are, doors that won't ever close again until you've worked through what's behind them.

But there's nothing wrong with doing things at your own pace. Getting clean is a very personal thing. And I cannot stress enough that what works for someone else might not work for you.

One of the most powerful words you can learn to say in any healing process is NO. No, I'm not ready; no, that doesn't feel right for me; or in any other context you feel it needs to be said. You can even extend it to a firm 'fuck off' if you feel the person is being particularly pushy. This is about you, and you're not there to be someone's project.

But if you do find yourself in a position where you feel ready to embark on such a journey, you're going to have to get yourself a sponsor.

That sounds easy enough, as the rooms are full of people who seem to know what they're talking about. But remember, this journey isn't just about how or why you used drugs. You're about to start clearing out your soul and exploring the essence of who you are. All those traumatic experiences and haunting guilt-ridden shameful secrets are about to come to light, and you can't share those with just anyone. It should be someone you feel comfortable with or naturally drawn to. And it should always be someone who has completed the programme themselves.

I know this sounds like a given, but I have heard of people who have either just started the programme or haven't done it at all trying to sponsor someone else. I know, it's ridiculous. But these were people from a different fellowship, so I'm not sure if that is something they endorse or not.

Another mistake some make is to choose a sponsor because of their perceived status, or how well they're spoken about in the fellowship, or because of their clean time, or because they can quote the literature word for word without looking at the book.

As impressive as those things might be, it doesn't necessarily make them a good choice. Take your time, watch how people conduct themselves, listen to what they share and how they speak about others. Find someone you're suited to and, most importantly, someone you feel you can trust.

I chose my sponsor because we'd had similar experiences, and I felt that he spoke honestly as opposed to just saying things to impress other people. When I asked him to become my sponsor, he actually tried to talk me out of it and suggested I pick someone else. Then we met for coffee, and I explained my reasons for asking him in the first place. Only then did he agree to become my sponsor. Although something told he had already made his mind up. He had brought a notepad and his own copy of the working guide, which he was allowing me to borrow… and he hadn't brought them for nothing.

Although some of my beliefs may have changed, there's no denying that the 12-Steps programme is a great place for any addict to begin exploring themselves and why they used. In fact, I think most people – not just addicts – could benefit from doing some variation of it, even if it's just to gain a better understanding of who they are, and to help them unburden themselves of things that no longer serve them.

I had my books, I had my sponsor, and 'recovery' was possible… if I could just see it through.

THE INTRODUCTORY STEPS

If I haven't made it clear enough already, the programme is a massive undertaking, so I think it would be easier for us all if I broke it down into sections.

Let's call Steps One-Three the introductory steps, as they introduce you to the ideas and principles of the 12-Steps. But I also want to talk about the kind of language that's used. The whole programme is a gentle step-by-step affirmation process: We admitted; We came to believe; We made a decision. Just like places, words are powerful, and these words give you a sense of ownership and empowerment. They help to make you feel proactive, as though you're finally taking charge of your situation.

This is also when you really begin to establish that trusting relationship with your sponsor and start to get comfortable with the whole God and higher power thing. You also have to start getting comfortable making yourself vulnerable with another person, writing out your thoughts, feelings, and experiences, then sharing them with someone else.

The concept of God is a recurring theme throughout the whole process, and anyone who says that God has nothing to do with the programme either hasn't done it or didn't do it properly. God can be one of the biggest obstacles; it's something a lot of people struggle with. But there really is no avoiding it.

Something I really struggled with wasn't just making myself vulnerable, but the thought of making myself vulnerable with another man, having intimate conversations about my feelings and sharing my darkest secrets. I had been around men all my life and, aside from my brother, they had all hurt me, abused me, or generally let me down in some way. So, I only saw other men as a threat. I didn't trust them.

But my wee Mammy never raised herself a shitebag. I knew what I had signed up for and that there were going to be tough challenges.

Not trusting other men was one of the first things I shared when I started writing and talking about what frightened and made me uncomfortable.

Getting used to sharing your feelings is only part of it, though. You need to get used to sitting with these feelings, too. We all know that when it comes to emotional healing, talking is the best cure. But there isn't always someone there. You can call or phone your higher power all you want, but that only works if there someone on the other end to answer.

At the end of the day, when the meetings are over, the front door shuts behind you, and your sponsor can't answer your calls, it's just you. Sometimes you don't have a choice and you just have to get comfortable with being uncomfortable. But you need to remember that no matter how unpleasant or overwhelming it might be, it's only temporary.

My willingness and enthusiasm got me through Steps One and Two, and I flew through them without really having to question anything. I spoke openly about my fears and what addiction meant to me, and I was happy to trust the process.

Then we hit the first bump in the road – Step Three, which is where the God card first comes into play. 'We made a decision to turn our will and our lives over to God, as we understood Him.' Up until this point, we had been swerving the whole God thing and focusing on the higher power bit. Now I was being asked to turn my will over to a God I didn't even believe in.

My sponsor could tell he was going to have a hard time convincing me that God was real. So, being the clever bastard that he is, we started talking about luck instead.

He asked if there had ever been a time when I'd felt like I had been saved from something, or been in some situation where the outcome could have been disastrous but turned out not to be.

And yes, of course there fucking was. I had been using for most of my life, so of course there had been some tricky situations and poor life choices that I had somehow managed to wriggle out of. He was smart, though, as he had a follow-up question. What about the times I didn't wriggle out? Were there times when things just seemed to happen in my favour?

I didn't have an answer for that. I had survived things I really shouldn't have. Sharing dirty needles in toilets with people I knew had hepatitis and not giving a fuck, for one thing. And I've been knocked down four times – sounds unbelievable, but it's true. So far, I've been hit by two cars, a tram, and a quad bike, and never once ended up in hospital. I was even set on fire once. I slipped into gouch on jellies. For the non-space travellers amongst you, jellies were capsules filled with temazepam linctus. They were originally prescribed as a sleeping tablet but were discontinued because of the amount of drug deaths they contributed to in the late 80s and early 90s. After they were discontinued, Glasgow saw an influx of street jellies in the late 90s, and they are similar to the street valium now being sold in Scotland, and no doubt in other places. A so-called friend thought it would be funny to set my jumper on fire with the tin of lighter gas I had been buzzing. A fireball shot up my back and filled the room with smell of burning hair, but amazingly there wasn't a mark on me.

The one lucky escape that really stuck out in my mind had nothing to do with avoiding personal injury. It was about how a much younger me had miraculously avoided spending time in prison.

At the time I was eighteen and living in a hostel called Elm House, formerly known as the Vegas Palace, just off Blackpool's north shore. A big guy from Greenock moved in after being released from prison, and as most Scottish boys tend to stick together down south, it wasn't long before me and this guy were out selling heroin together. I say selling it together, but he was really the one selling it. I was just the one stupid enough to carry it for him, with my only reward being free heroin.

One night we were out doing our thing and had just come out of an alleyway, after selling a couple of bags to two fellow opiate enthusiasts, when we were stopped by the police. They had been watching and decided to let us get round the corner before letting us know they were there. Before I knew what was going on I was face-to-face with two uniformed police officers with fifteen bags of heroin in my pocket.

I was pretty certain that I was fucked and would definitely be looking at a prison sentence… but they never found them. They searched me and the other guy then arrested him for having what they referred to as a large sum of money that he couldn't explain. He was taken to the police station for a strip search, and I walked away with fifteen bags of heroin on me. I still don't know how they missed it. Was it some sort of divine intervention? Or was I just lucky enough to have been searched by two incompetent police officers? Or maybe the two incompetent police officers were my divine intervention? I wasn't sure.

One thing I was sure of was that I didn't believe in wee beardy men living in the clouds performing miracles and judging people's morals. I certainly had no time for organised religion, and I think that was the problem. The only God I knew was the god of one religion or another.

The title of Step Three was very clear, though. This was about a God of my understanding, not about me trying to understand other people's idea of who or what God is.

By then I had already begun to explore yoga and reiki, and some of the spiritual teachings that came with them. I had discovered the concept of something they call the God body, the idea that everything in the universe is one big mass of interconnected intelligent energy. That sounded a bit like abstract physics – not that I know much about physics! – but it made more sense to me than the wee beardy man story.

Then there was the question of will and whether my idea of God and the programme's idea of God were the same thing.

It might say a God of your understanding. But it also says to turn your will and your life over to 'Him', not 'it'. All the way through the programme God is referred to as He or Him, where the A.A. founders Bill W and Dr Bob talk about a traditional biblical form of God. (William Grifith Wilson and Robert Holburn Smith were the two men who founded Alcoholics Anonymous as a global fellowship in 1935.)

Ok, so what was the difference, as long as you had a God? In my case, the difference was that it sounded like we were talking about the old-school creator God. For me, that made things even more complicated. According to the religious people, our biblical creator didn't make mistakes, and we were created in His image. But if that was the case, and He was the one who created me, it was God's will that I was an addict.

If I didn't want to be an addict anymore, surely that was my will. So, whose will did I follow: mine or God's? It was all very confusing; none of it made any sense. When I spoke to my sponsor about it, he just said I was over-thinking it.

Not wanting to quit, but not sure if I should continue, I decided to stick with it and only keep the parts of the programme that I felt made sense and leave the parts that didn't.

NOW I'M AN ACTION MAN

Determination had carried me over some tall hurdles, and I had managed to establish a trusting relationship with my sponsor, discovered an idea of God that made sense to me, and decided that I was going to see this through to the end. However, I kept the taking what worked and leaving what didn't bit to myself. No-one needed to know about that, and if I had told my sponsor he might have said there was no point in continuing. I only wanted to do this once, and I knew that if I stopped, I probably wouldn't have started again.

Moving on, Steps Four-Nine are what they call the action steps. This is where all the real work takes place, but it's also where people usually bail out if they're not quite ready to face themselves.

This is where we face all those demons of shame and guilt, the ones that haunt our thoughts and deprive us of sleep. We pull them out of the shadows and put them in a cage that's strong enough to hold them. They never really go away; they'll always be there to rear their heads every now and then, but once you've faced them, they no longer have any power. They get a lot quieter, and after enough time you even learn to laugh at them.

The reason people struggle so much with Step Four is because it's not just about how or why you used drugs. It's about you as a person. The title says it all: 'We made a searching and fearless moral inventory of ourselves.' Tell me that title alone isn't enough to make you shit yourself. It covers everything – and I do mean everything – you're ashamed of. Violence, sexual conduct, the people you've fucked over, people you resent because they've fucked you over. It all comes out here.

If you do make it this far, my advice is to leave nothing out, no matter how guilty, shameful, or embarrassed it might make you feel.

I felt real shame at speaking openly about how being addicted to pornography at such a young age had really affected me. I was comfortable to speak about everything else, but not that. And ironically, during Step Four porn and food became my main coping strategies. Not together, though. Not that I'm judging. It would just be too messy for my wee OCD brain to cope with, but you do whatever makes you happy… provided you can do it without intentionally hurting someone else, and everyone's signed the consent form.

When it comes to Step Four, we all need a coping strategy, and as long as that strategy isn't smack, crack, or Frosty Jack's, you're doing fine. You're literally going through the process of tearing yourself apart emotionally so that you can be rebuilt, so cut yourself some slack.

Aside from the porn addiction stuff that I held back to speak about another day, I poured my soul out in this step. I spoke about how I had robbed my friends' houses after they had been good enough to take me in and feed me. How I had robbed and manipulated my poor wee mum and affected her mental health so badly that she nearly had a breakdown and was forced to turn her back on me. That I had let my brother down and bullied him because of my own insecurities, and hadn't protected or guided him like an older brother should. I took things out on him that weren't his fault, even if I didn't mean to. Or I was so out of it that I didn't even remember doing it.

A lot of times it's better not to remember some of the things we've done. I certainly have some memories I wish I could wipe clean.

But sometimes not remembering is worse, like when people tell you their own recollection of what you did after you'd blacked out, so your head fills in the empty spaces.

I wasn't consistently violent, but when I was I was *really* violent. I think it stemmed from all those years of repressed anger while I was being bullied at school, although I'm not trying to make excuses.

You can't make a wrong thing right, but there is a difference between justification and explanation. I've tried my best to understand why I made some of my more questionable choices, not justify why it was ok for me to have made those choices in the first place.

As I said, there are different types of anger – implicit and explicit. When my anger was implicit, I would cut myself; when it was explicit, I took it out on the world. I went through a phase in my early twenties when I felt I had to prove to the world that I wasn't a victim any longer. Instead of avoiding fights, I went looking for them. And on the odd occasion the fight came looking for me, it sometimes ended badly.

Once I crawled home after a particularly heavy weekend, with the genuine intention of going to bed. When I walked through the door, my mum's first words were to stay calm and not overreact, which was usually a sure-fire sign that I was going to lose my shit. Apparently, my brother's girlfriend claimed she had been sexually assaulted by a friend's dad at a house party. She said she had fallen asleep on the couch and woken up with the guy on top of her. I'm saying apparently because, let's face it, I wasn't there so I don't really know what happened.

I went to the guy's house, but he wouldn't come out. I was shouting at him from the street, he was shouting from the window, and nothing happened. A few phone calls later, though, the girl's stepdad paid him a visit, so there was no need for me to take it any further. As far as I was concerned, it was over with. But later that night the guy came at me in the street, and I ended up fighting with him while my mum was rolling about on the floor with his girlfriend.

Amid all this carnage, the guy came at me with a bottle, so I took out a knife. In those days, I rarely left the house without one. I tried to blind him but, luckily, I missed his eye, though the guy's face was a mess.

None of that had anything to do with my brother or his girlfriend, or the things this guy was supposed to have done. It was about me taking my anger out on the world, and me proving to myself that I was no longer a victim.

Each Step has different parts or sections. For the most part, Step Four was about my behaviour, how that behaviour had affected other people, and essentially how it had affected me. But there was another part – a part about how I felt about other people's behaviour. And this was all about my resentments. And because I began to understand them in a way I never thought I could, I found myself forgiving someone I thought I'd never forgive.

I had hated my dad since childhood. I saw him as a selfish alcoholic bully who took his issues out on his family, and a man who threw us out on the street after he and my mum split up. The anger and resentment I carried from that was a big part of my justification for my using drugs. I believed that what my life became was partly, if not mostly, his fault. Or at least that was what I used to think.

Those same old excuses weren't good enough any longer, though. I had started to realise that other people had been through a lot worse than me yet hadn't ended up living the way I did.

My excuses about not being enough were the precursor to me being clean now, even if it didn't happen straight away.

When I got clean and started talking about my issues, I realised how similar my dad and I actually were. Like me, he had been lost in a world he didn't understand and felt things he could neither interpret or express. The only difference was that I had found a way out and begun to pull my life together in a way he never could, though he did try. He tried not drinking, he tried going to meetings, but he just wasn't strong enough. For the first time in my life, I felt sorry for him. All that anger and resentment I'd felt for so long was replaced with sympathy. Sympathy for a man who probably spent years torturing himself for mistakes he felt he could never make up for. In the end, he died on the floor alone, with a glass of whisky still in his hand.

I had survived the dreaded Step Four and been brave enough to face my monsters – well, most of them – and was ready to move on.

Steps Five, Six, and Seven are pretty much just one big step, as they're all about the same thing and just feed into one another. First, we admit to God, to ourselves, and to another human being the exact nature of our wrongs. Then we become entirely ready to have God remove all our defects of character. And finally, we humbly ask God to remove all our shortcomings.

It starts to sound a bit more biblical now, doesn't it? I told you God was a recurring theme. And to me this definitely sounds like the good old-fashioned, old-worldly God we all know and fear, the bringer of judgement and absolution. You know what? If God really does exist, I feel sorry for Him. He gets the blame for everything, and most of us only ever talk to Him with any real sincerity when we want something.

My sponsor's approach to the steps was a bit biblical, too. His way of helping me define the exact nature of my wrongs was to have me write out the seven deadly sins and think about how they applied to my own choices and behaviours. Then I had to write out the seven heavenly virtues to help me try and curb the parts of my life that I felt were unhealthy or unmanageable.

When you look at this loosely, and try not to think about the whole heaven and hell aspect, it sort of makes sense to use a set of positive actions to balance out what could be seen as negative ones. It all still just felt a little bit too religious for me, though. And did any of the things on either of these lists have to be specifically sinful or virtuous in the first place?

Yes, I had been lustful, greedy, and gluttonous. And anyone that's suffered from low self-esteem could say they'd been prideful because their ego had stepped in to save them for their lack of self-worth. But could a slothful day not be considered as a form of self-care after a sixty-hour week? And don't get me started on wrath and envy. Just swipe through your social media feed and you'll find those in abundance.

At the other end of the spectrum, was writing this stuff out not an example of me practising humility? I had already admitted that I needed help and taken it when it was offered, even when I didn't fully agree with the message that help was carrying. So, I'd say that was pretty fucking humble, wouldn't you? I had shared drugs with people that were rattling, and given money to people less fortunate than me, even when I was less than fortunate myself. That's charitable by anyone's standards.

And there were times in my life when my drug use had robbed me of my libido, so I didn't have sex or used pornography, which could be seen as a form of chastity.

My point is that things aren't all black and white, and for every so-called 'sin' in my life there was a virtue. To me these were all just aspects of being human. My only real issue was overindulgence, or an inability to self-regulate, or otherwise expressing these things in an unhealthy way. Even the so-called virtuous ones. After all, even charity can be problematic if it becomes an obsession we're compelled to act upon. And that is the very essence of all our addictive behaviours.

Once again, I was honest with my sponsor and told him exactly what I've just told you. I didn't see any of these things as defects in themselves; they were just aspects of being human. And as a thirty-five-year-old man, I certainly didn't want my lust to be removed, thank you very much, as I was pretty sure I was going to need that at some point.

So, we both agreed – my sponsor and I, that is, not God – that our lack of self-regulation was a real defect.

Recognising the real problem, though, created a problem of its own. How can someone begin to learn self-control after living without it for so long?

Well, you don't have to; it starts to happen on its own. While you're opening up and talking about all those shameful guilty secrets, you're redefining your moral compass and you start to understand how certain behaviours made or still make you feel.

I still make poor choices, act selfishly, and say inappropriate things that offend other people from time to time. And I'm fine with that. We're all fallible, and life would be boring if we all just agreed and didn't offend other people occasionally. But now I know when I've crossed the line, as it leaves a bitter taste in my mouth.

The old me wouldn't have given a fuck. But the new me does. It doesn't sit well with me, so when I cross the line, I have to fix it. Not just for the other person, but for myself, too. If I don't, it eats away at me.

Sometimes, it's even just about how I perceive the other person must have felt. I find myself apologising for something, and the other person doesn't have a clue what I'm talking about because they never even picked up on it. Like feeling as though I'm not paying attention to my mum when she's on the phone, because I'm scrolling through TikTok or swiping right on some dating site. She's that busy ranting that she's not even noticed that I'm not paying attention. Then when I phone back to apologise, she's confused because she doesn't know what I'm talking about. I guess it just shows that neither of us had the other's full attention. But at least my side of the street is clean. I didn't feel good about not listening to her, so I did what I could to make it right.

Then there are the times when I knew I had genuinely upset someone. I don't mean said something inappropriately funny, or disagreed with their opinion; I'm fine with that. I mean times where it seemed like I had discarded their feelings altogether, but that doesn't happen often and is rarely intentional.

Even then, though, my apology takes people by surprise. They're not used to meeting people who are that self-aware. And they're certainly not used to people who have the confidence to address their own faults face-to-face without trying to find some loose-fitting justification.

It's the same when someone offends or even attacks me in some way. Most people expect an angry or heightened emotional response, because that's what they're used to. Instead, I calmly call them out and ask them if that's honestly how they want to treat people. And most of the time they don't know how to respond.

Of course, it's different if the attack is physical, as any threat of real bodily harm changes the game completely. Thankfully, though, instances like that are few and far between, so it's best not thinking about it at all until it happens… if it ever does. And if it does, you usually have a chance to walk away before things get out of hand.

We're more than halfway through the action steps and it's time to put all that newfound self-awareness to good use. In Step Eight we make a list of all those we harmed, and prepare to make amends to them all. And in the same way as Steps Five, Six, and Seven go hand-in-hand, Step Four is directly connected to Step Eight, as you could no doubt tell by the title.

This is another one where the title alone is enough to give you the fear, but it's actually just a list of names. The real fear kicks in if you have to actually go and face these people, which is something you might not even have to do. You'll find out why later.

The list comprises all those people you fucked over and things you felt shameful about in Step Four, along with anything else that managed to bubble up to the surface while you were writing everything out.

Ok, so I lied. It's not just a list. Like everything else you've already written, it's another affirmation of change, and the key is in the title: 'We became willing.' You're not only sorry for the things you did, but you're willing to try and make up for them in whatever way possible. We can't undo the things we've done, but we can try to balance them out.

Step Eight isn't a particularly big step and is pretty much self-explanatory, and it leads us nicely into Step Nine: 'We make direct amends wherever possible, except when it would cause harm to ourselves of others.'

When I spoke to other people about this step, I found out how lucky I really was to have picked a decent sponsor, because some of them take this step too far. Other guys told me that their sponsor had made them go into shops they had stolen from and apologise to the manger, or even hand themselves in for outstanding warrants. That is fucking ridiculous, if you ask me, and they clearly didn't read the title properly or just decided to ignore it altogether.

If you did have a sponsor like that and you did put yourself in a precarious position during this step, with all due respect, you, my friend, are a mug. I couldn't give a single fuck what my sponsor said. There was no chance of me knocking on doors to say sorry for robbing someone's house or sleeping with their girlfriend, or walking into a police station and asking them to arrest me.

Luckily my sponsor was a little more level-headed. Anyone with any sense knows that 'sorry' is only a word, and it means nothing. It's a shield people use when they've been caught doing something they shouldn't. Or when they want someone else to forgive them and fix their feelings because they don't want to feel guilty.

The only real apology is showing someone that you've changed. Although sometimes direct action, or letting people see the new you, just isn't possible. This is Glasgow, good auld Glesga toon.

And if I had gone to those people's houses to apologise, it could have ended badly for me or for them, and ended up doing even more damage. Sometimes when you weigh it up, it's just not worth it. And sometimes the only real amends we can make is amending the choices we make.

That doesn't only mean not making the same choices again; it means making better choices that might lead us to do some good in the world.

There were, however, some amends that I had to do face-to-face. To my mum and my brother. I had to sit down with them, not so much to apologise but to try and explain why something happened, and to give them the chance to express how they felt. This wasn't just about me; it was about them, too. I wasn't the only one healing. They were healing, too.

The conversations with them were relatively easy, given the situation. I wasn't stupid; I knew what I had put them through, and I had a good idea of how they felt about it. But I think they were just happy I was no longer using and seemed to be finally getting my life together. I owed amends to my brother's kids as well, but they were too young to fully understand the situation, never mind have a conversation about it. My eldest niece did say something that stuck with me, though, when she told me, 'Uncle Tony, you're a lot lighter now that you've started doing yoga. You're not as dark as you used to be.'

I had taken up practising yoga when I was seven days clean., but I still don't know what she meant – if it was my tone or my energy. She just knew something about me had changed and decided to tell me as simply and eloquently as an eight-year-old could.

My amends to her and her sister was to be the best uncle and role model I could be. I have no idea if I've managed that; only my nieces could answer that question. But I've done my best.

So far there was no-one on the list that I didn't already expect to be there when I first undertook this journey. But you might remember in Step Four I realised I had to make amends to someone else – my dad. But how could you make peace with someone who was no longer here?

By the time I had reached Step Nine, I had been clean for just over a year, and I had established a daily yoga practice which encouraged me to explore my own ideas about spirituality a little more. Following the idea of God being the interconnected energy of the entire universe, I accepted that some type of divine guidance and support might exist, even if I didn't understand it. And my philosophy even now is that a force we could never fully comprehend guides us to where we need to be, even if it sometimes feels like we're in the wrong place.

I started doing voluntary work for the same organisation as my brother – the North East Recovery Community (or NERC, as they called themselves) – partly to give something back after taking for so long, and also because it gave me something constructive to do with my time. But mostly I did it so that my brother could see the effort I was willing to put in and how much I had changed.

I was very vocal and enthusiastic about my yoga practice and my newfound spiritual ideas. I prefer to call them 'ideas' than 'beliefs', as they're very rigid and hard to change while beliefs are more pliable.

NERC wanted to introduce new types of therapies and offer a more holistic range of services, so they had me attuned as a reiki practitioner, which was a technique I was already very curious about. A lot of people are unsure about energy work or energy healing, if they don't dismiss it altogether. But I think that's mostly because they've never experienced it. If they had, they might be less sceptical. Over the years I've delivered hundreds of treatments, working with people that had addiction or mental health issues, or both. Because as interconnected as they may often be, they're not the same thing.

Most of these people were sceptical about reiki and only opted for the treatment in the first place because it was free. Most of the time I think they mistook it for some type of massage. Then, when they were in the treatment room and found out it wasn't, they thought, *Fuck it, I'm here now so I might as well*. Yet every single one of those people experienced something they didn't expect, and they all felt better after their session. We're talking about the same intelligent energy that flows through the entire universe, and you don't have to believe in it for it to work.

While I was being attuned as a reiki master – I know it sounds a little pretentious, but it's the accepted terminology – we spoke in the training about the idea of ascended masters and teachers. These were a mix of gods, saints, and supernatural beings, and real people who had died and passed on but existed in the universe as a form of conscious energy. Reiki practitioners are taught that they can channel these entities to work through while they deliver treatments.

Me being me, I looked at it from a scientific perspective. Human beings are another expression of that same energy, and physics tells us that energy is a constant. It can't be destroyed; it can only change form. So, as far-fetched as it may sound, to me when someone died it was entirely possible for them to exist somewhere in the cosmos as a form of conscious energy.

This may sound ludicrous, but it's genuinely what I think, and I've yet to meet anyone with an argument logical enough to change my mind. In fact, when I explain it to other people, it often makes them rethink their own ideas of what might be possible. Personally, I find the idea rather comforting, as it means that no-one ever truly leaves. They continue to exist out there somewhere in a form we can't fully perceive. And, if I'm right, it could offer a more tangible explanation for 'divine intervention'. Maybe it's not God, but ancestors and loved ones that have passed on, stepping in to help us when we need it most.

If that was the case, my dad was still out there somewhere, and that meant there was no reason I couldn't speak to him. Being who

I am, I wasn't just going to sit in the house and talk to the celling; there had to be some semblance of ceremony.

I went to the garden of remembrance in the crematorium and tried to find the plaque with his name on it, but there was nothing. It was as if he had been wiped from the planet. So, I picked a bench in a quiet spot and just spoke. As ceremonial as I wanted it to be, I hadn't planned what I wanted to say. I opened my mouth and let the words come out on their own.

I told him that he had been selfish and made choices that had affected not only me, but the whole family. I said I'd spent my childhood scared of him, and the rest of my life hatefully resenting him. Then I told him that now I understood, and that my own experience had helped me to understand what made him the way he was and the choices he had made. I also confessed that I was more like him than I was ever willing to admit. The only difference being that I hadn't been silly or selfish enough to have children when it was clear I couldn't even manage my own life, and that I had eventually managed to get my life together in a way that he never could.

I finished off by telling him that no-one deserved to die the way he did, feeling alone and unloved and tortured by the ghosts of their past. And I forgave him and asked him to forgive me. I had a set of prayer beads looped around my wrist that I had been wearing for months. And as I was leaving the garden, I took them off and took out a year-clean keyring, which glows in the dark for those of you that have never seen one. I hooked the keyring onto the beads then tied them to a tree. Giving him my first-year clean keyring was my way of finally making peace between us.

This, however, is where things started to get a bit weird. On the way home I was naturally still feeling very emotional, so I went into the supermarket because, as we know, food is one of my main coping mechanisms. While I was looking for something to shield me from my feelings, the Ugly Kid Joe cover version of the Cat

Stevens' song 'Cats in the Cradle' came on. The song is about a man who feels emotionally neglected by his father, who then feels abandoned by his own son in later life. And the man realises that his son has grown up to be just like him.

You can think what you want, but hearing that song at that moment felt to me like my dad telling me he had heard me. If he was out there somewhere, and divine intervention was the loved ones that had passed on looking after us, why couldn't they send us messages, too? Since then, every year on Father's Day and his birthday, I write him a letter, burn sage, bang drums, and play that song for him.

MAINTENANCE

I had put my big boy pants on and made it through the action steps. After hearing all the steps and what's involved, you might understand why some people tap out and never go back to it again. You might also possibly have a bit more respect for the ones who manage to see it through. And if you still think it sounds easy, try it for yourself then get back to me.

I had sacrificed over a year of my life to do what you've just read, and it was worth it. I had unburdened my soul – well, mostly – and felt like I was becoming a completely new person. I was Glasgow's very own Andy Dufresne, the guy that swam through a river of shit and came out clean. And that is how someone should feel if they've done the programme properly.

If I wanted to continue to be the new me, though, I would need tools to help me maintain everything I had worked so hard to build. Going back to the earlier CBT reference, I had identified where I was and worked out where I wanted to be, while talking about my issues. Now it was time to continue to cultivate the self-awareness I had already developed and to fine-tune the tools I had learned to use along the way to help keep me and my life balanced.

Step Ten is designed to help you cultivate even more self-awareness: 'We continue to take personal inventory and when we were wrong promptly admitted it.'

I don't think the title does this step justice, if I'm honest, because it's about a lot more than apologising when we're wrong. On a much broader spectrum it's about recognising how all our behaviours and interactions affect us and other people. The clever people at the fellowship have even made a little pamphlet for it. I've never used one myself, but they should be available at meetings if you decide that meetings are for you.

I've said it before and I'll say it again, everything is interconnected even if the connection isn't obvious. Have you ever woken up feeling like shit for no apparent reason? Or started obsessively over-thinking about something you did or said, or what someone said or did to you? Somewhere, somehow, you've been triggered. You've either triggered yourself or been triggered by someone or something else.

The word trigger is thrown around a lot these days. It's become a buzz word, something people say when someone disagrees with them or says something they find offensive. But that's not what it means at all. You can go around using buzz words to censor other people just because you disagree with how they express themselves. Unless, of course, they're attacking you directly in some way or another.

To be triggered means you've had an unconditional, and sometimes overwhelming, emotional response to some type of stimulus. You don't decide when you're triggered and when you're not; the trigger does. Sometimes the things that trigger us are obvious. Then there are times where there's so much stimulus, or our interactions seem so inconsequential, that we're not sure how or why they've affected us.

I started to handle my situations differently, not because someone else told me I had to, but because the new me wanted to. I learned how honesty and ownership could change how I felt about things. If I said something that had genuinely upset someone or said something I felt was inappropriate, I apologised.

Note that I'm saying things which I felt were inappropriate. We can't be going around apologising because we've expressed our opinion or offended someone by disagreeing with them. I'm talking about the times where I've tried to make myself feel better by taking my emotions out on someone else, and that leads us nicely back to managing triggers. For example, if I'm in a situation that has made me feel anxious and I've then snapped at someone. Or there was someone I was attracted to, and I tried to show off and be funny by making a comment about someone else that came across as snide.

Luckily this sort of behaviour was happening when the old me and the new me were still getting to know each other, so it rarely happens now, if at all. I still offend some people just by being me, though, but that sounds more like a them problem than a me problem. We live our lives for ourselves, not for everyone else.

It's the same when I feel like someone has directed something towards me that I didn't deserve or isn't mine to carry. A quiet word in private is usually more effective than an emotional, or in some cases even aggressive, outburst. If you're ever in this position, remember to be patient with yourself. Self-awareness and development aren't set goals; it's an ongoing practice, and I'm still trying to get it right.

In Step Eleven, it turns out that even though Bill W, Dr Bob, and I may have differing opinions when it comes to God, we have a similar take on useful tools and coping strategies. 'We seek through prayer and meditation to improve our conscious contact with God as we understood Him, praying only for knowledge of His will and the power to carry that out.'

Fuck me, that was a long one. You must be breathless after reading that. Like most people presumably, by this point I just wanted this thing done. But the God's will thing was still niggling me. Even if God was real, could we – a race whose existence counts as less than a second in the vast time of the cosmos – possibly understand the will of a supreme being who had existed since before the dawn of time? The answer is most likely no, which would make consciously carrying out that being's will extremely difficult.

As for prayer, does it really have to be spiritual or religious? Could it not be seen as another form of affirmation?

Most of us pray for outcomes, things we want or don't want, that we see as being out of our control, and occasionally we pray when we're very grateful – if we remember, that is.

Don't you think it's coincidental that people who never believed in any God, or denied their existence altogether, suddenly turn to them when their lives fall apart? Or when they've been caught doing something they shouldn't have done? To me, prayer is just another way of affirming what you want or what you don't.

As for the meditation part, that can be spiritual, but no-one says it has to be. It doesn't have to be complicated either. I was meditating before I even started the programme. However, it went hand-in-hand with the yoga and reiki, and it was a big part of my routine. It became a regular practice just like going to the yoga studio, chanting mantras, and smudging my house with sage. Obviously, I'm not suggesting you start chanting and wafting smoke about your house with feathers. Sitting in silence, focusing on your breath, trying not to let your thoughts bother you, is challenging enough.

As a mindfulness facilitator, I know that some people still have the wrong idea about meditation. They think you have to sit with your legs crossed and make funny shapes with your fingers, and that everyone who meditates has mastered the art of silencing their mind. While certain postures and mudras – the funny finger shapes – can be part of some meditative practice, they're not a requirement. And no-one, not even monks sitting in the Buddhist temples of the Himalayas, have managed to silence their minds completely.

For the most part, sitting in a posture that's relatively comfortable – or even better, lying down (my favourite) – while you focus on your breath, that's enough... at least in the beginning. Don't run before you can walk.

The less complicated you make meditation in the beginning, the more likely you are to make it a regular part of your life. It's not so much about connecting with God, and more about connecting with yourself. And I've found that sitting with myself and connecting with my breath for just five minutes can change my whole day. It gives me space to reset my mind and helps me to process whatever might be going on in my life at the time. It's not about silencing your thoughts but about peacefully accepting them without them becoming a running narrative. And the longer you sustain a regular practice the quieter your mind will become.

And now here we are at the final step in the journey. Step Twelve, having a spiritual awakening as a result of these steps: 'We tried to carry this message to other addicts and to practise these principles in all our affairs.'

A spiritual awakening sounds like a big statement, and at the time I thought it sounded a bit arrogant. But now when I think about it, it was true.

I had found a god that made sense to me; developed spiritual ideas and regular practices that helped me understand and develop those ideas further; I had learned to understand and empathise with myself, which helped me do the same with others; I'd made peace with my past and learned to forgive myself and the people who had negatively impacted on my life; and in the process I'd grown into a new version of me that I had never dreamed could possibly exist. Was it an awakening? Yes. Was there a spiritual element involved? Definitely. Even if it did seem a bit conventional, it didn't matter. All that mattered was that it made sense to me.

'Carrying this message to other addicts in all my affairs' basically meant promoting the fellowship's ideology and sponsoring other people, but I wasn't sure I could do that.

I had completed the programme, and my life was so much better. But there was just so much I'd had to push past, so much of the programme that didn't make sense to me. I wasn't completely convinced that addiction was a disease, or that powerlessness fully relinquished my responsibility over my choices. Then there was all the stuff about God's will.

I had found me, but not answers – or not the answers I wanted, anyway. So, I didn't feel I could spread the message or sponsor anyone else while I was thinking like that. It would be hypocritical. I decided that instead of carrying a message that didn't completely make sense, I would keep asking questions in the hope that I found something that did.

OUTSIDE HELP

Some people go through the programme, accept that their addiction was a disease, keep going to meetings… and that becomes their way of life.

But by now I think we've all established that I am not that guy.

There was no denying my life was in a much better place, and for the first time for as long as I could remember my head was quiet. No vultures pecking at my brain, stealing any moments of peace I managed to find.

The sleep paralysis had stopped, and I was sleeping right through the night. Dreaming was another thing my drug use had seemed quite content to take from me. I didn't dream when I was using, or I had no memory of it if I did.

Now I got to wake up and have a coffee and a cigarette like a normal person. Funnily enough, that's what I said the first Christmas after I got clean.

I was at my voluntary work and one of the guys asked what I was up to later. I told him I was going home to put my tree up. The guy seemed confused and asked me why I was bothering to put a tree up when I didn't have any kids. So, I said quite proudly that at that time of year normal people would wrestle a six-foot plastic tree out of its box and stick it up in their living room. And now that I was a normal person, that's exactly what I planned to do.

Of course, we know that there is no such thing as a normal

person, but it was just another way for me to affirm how much I had changed. I had spoiled enough Christmases and didn't plan on ruining anymore. So, there's been a Christmas tree in my living room every year since.

Life hasn't all been sunshine and rainbows, though. All the way through the programme my mind was relatively still, and the disturbing, intrusive thoughts that I associated with my using had stopped. But then they started coming back and were louder than ever. I couldn't understand it! I wasn't using, and I had been mostly honest with my sponsor, so why was this happening? These weren't thoughts of using, which was only to be expected, but they were much darker. Thoughts of violence, and even sexual violence, were pecking at my mind like crows on a battlefield.

At least if they had been enjoyable thoughts, I would have been able to process them. But these thoughts were disturbing and left me riddled with anxiety.

The advice would always be to speak about it. But how do you even begin to tell someone you're having those kinds of thoughts?

Ironically, by that stage in the journey I had been trained as a mindfulness facilitator, leading support groups for people with mental health and addiction issues, to show them how to use meditation to cope with intrusive thoughts and manage their triggers. But sometimes I would be sitting there leading a group while my head was so loud it drowned out the rest of the room. I felt like I was in a darkened cave and only remembered where I was when someone asked me a question. Sometimes they had to ask more than once.

They kept asking me to lead the groups, though, which just goes to show that people can hide their issues even if they feel overwhelmed by them. On any given day you could be interacting with someone who's fighting a battle so well hidden that no-one else can see it. That kinda makes you re-evaluate how you treat people, doesn't it? You never know what someone else might be going through, so always try and be patient with people unless they give you a genuine reason not to be.

As I said, what really puggled my brain was that I had always associated my uncontrollable mind with my drug use. So, I'd expected that when the using stopped, the thoughts would stop, too. Turns out I was wrong. I tried telling myself the same things I would tell the people in my groups, that thoughts were only thoughts and that most of them were repetitive nonsense.

The human brain processes seventy thousand thoughts every day, most of which live in the deep unknown of our subconscious and only bubble up to the surface in the form of desires, judgements, or opinions we sometimes never fully understand. They can be harmless, exciting, even arousing. But others can be damaging, like the repetitive nonsense that tells us we're not good enough, or less than we really are, or even seem to make us believe we're something we're not, never were, or aren't anymore.

The more I wrestled with my mind, the louder it became, and at times I would pace the floor and argue with myself. I became so consumed by it that it got to stage where I would argue with myself out loud in the street, forgetting that other people could see me. And I mean a full-scale argument, hands flailing and everything. Anyone who saw me must have thought I'd managed to escape from a locked ward on a hospital wing.

Truth be told, my mum and I now agree that there were some stages during my using when I should really have been sectioned, but she just couldn't bring herself to do it. And at this stage of the journey, you would have thought I was still on drugs.

I had held onto those thoughts and argued with them for so long that they started to feel like a bubble underneath my skull. I was convinced they were going to be there for the rest of my life.

Once again, my go-where guided approach to my new life led me to where I needed to be. And my new god, the intelligent interconnected energy of the universe, seemed to know how to help me.

The powers-that-be – well, Glasgow City Council – had just introduced the elevate project, offering volunteers like me a chance to gain new qualifications. I managed to get a place on something called the COSCA (Counselling and Psychotherapy in Scotland) course, which provides an introduction to counselling skills and approaches.

I think there were ten of us, all with histories of addiction, volunteering in different recovery networks throughout the city. And the course was hosted at the GCA (Glasgow Council on Alcohol) – the first time they had ever facilitated the course where the whole group had a history of long-term addiction.

It wasn't counselling in the conventional sense, as in just going to a therapist and talking about your problems. We were learning to counsel other people as we counselled each other. So, we didn't just get to speak about our issues – both in the usual way of therapist and client, and as a group – but got to learn more about the possible reasons behind those issues. It was a lot more in-depth and made a lot more sense than being told we had a disease we were powerless over.

If, like me, you had finished the programme and were left with more questions than answers, counselling – or outside help, as it is often referred to in fellowships – is a nice way of continuing that journey of self-exploration and understanding.

THE INNER VIKING

I had convinced myself that I was going to go into this being willing and open, but the truth was there were still some things I felt I shouldn't or couldn't speak about, and I was determined to keep those things to myself. However, as the days and weeks went on, I found more and more that the course work, and the conversations in the group counselling sessions, were strongly reflecting my own inner struggle. So, I started to talk about my inner struggle, albeit in a roundabout way.

The course was facilitated by a wee guy called Neil McAully, who had a lot of experience with addicts and people with eating disorders, and he really knew his stuff.

One morning at the check-in, the guy sitting next to me was saying that he had been single for a while, and that he had recently started watching porn again.

He said the reason he had stopped was because he found that the images he was watching were becoming more extreme, the girls were getting younger, and the scenarios were becoming more questionable. He wasn't watching anything illegal; it could all be found on multiple sites online for free, and I know that because the stuff I was watching was very similar. He spoke about how it was affecting him emotionally and admitted he didn't feel good about himself.

This sparked off a group discussion about human nature and

morality. Neil said that everyone had what he called the Inner Viking, the part of us that just wants to rape, pillage, and plunder. It's ok, you don't have to admit it. I know it's there and it's a perfectly normal part of being human. What we all like to try and forget is that, as advanced as we are, we are really just hairless apes. By our very nature we are savage creatures. And that it's only though our emotional evolution as a society that we've learned that certain things are wrong. However, that savage part still lives inside us as our shadow self. Or our Inner Viking, which is the term I now often use myself.

It's the part of us that likes violent movies and kinky sex, which most of us will never admit to because we fear being judged… without realising that the people we fear may judge us have similar thoughts and urges to our own.

It's that little voice that suggests that we do things we know are unacceptable. And of course, behind it are those thoughts that disturb us and seem to test the very nature of who we are.

REVISITING STEP FOUR

I had been living with all this carnage in my head and carrying the shame of it for so long that my brain felt like it was too big for my skull. Then one day I couldn't hold onto it anymore. I had to let it out, and there was only one person in the world I trusted enough to let them hear it.

I hadn't spoken with my sponsor in months, which isn't unusual when people have finished the programme. But he already knew most of my secrets and had helped me work through them, so maybe it was time he heard some more. And when he did... he laughed. He fucking laughed! There I was, sharing the darkest part of my soul, and this bastard thought it was funny.

And that's because it was.

Because I had never spoken about it, I had no idea that everyone had similar thoughts. I had learned that we all have fucked-up thoughts, but for some reason I just didn't think anyone else's were as fucked-up as mine. We do like to think we're special, remember. And in a world where people make horror films about sex offenders, with razor blades for fingers that invade children's dreams, I still thought my mind was sicker than anyone else's. Guess I just wasn't paying attention.

The first thing my sponsor advised was to go along to a meeting. I hadn't been to one in months and had no plans of returning anytime soon. After all, I didn't agree with the ideology, they had gurus that didn't seem to know anything, and I felt that the things I needed to talk about could only be said one-to-one, not shared with a group.

My sponsor and I decided we would treat it like an extension of Step Four, which essentially it was, because it was all the stuff I had kept to myself the first time round. All the stuff I had glossed over and never really spoken about.

We didn't do the whole step, though, and I never even picked up the book. I didn't have to. I knew exactly what I wanted to speak about, and I wrote it all down, which was difficult enough on its own.

I would always walk to my sponsor's house when I was sharing step work, so that I could get my head in the right space. Then I'd walk home afterwards to help me process everything and decompress. I always took emotional support cakes, too. People might say it's only talking, but this kind of emotionally-charged talking can be exhausting. So, I'm usually grateful for the calories.

I shared my thoughts, he shared some of his, and my tears turned to laughter, both at the ridiculousness of my thoughts and the fact that I had taken them so seriously that it had overwhelmed my life and made me question who I was. After that, I started paying more attention to other people, the things they said and even did in some cases. I thought, *If that's the part of you that you show to the world, I don't even want to think about the things you have hidden.* They seemed to treat their shadow with a humorous disregard because they knew they were essentially a good person, whereas I had taken mine seriously and thought that part of me defined who I was.

While other people had the same kind of thoughts and never doubted themselves the way I did, they seemed to instinctively know that that part of them wasn't an honest representation of who they were. But I didn't; I thought it was those thoughts that defined who I was. They were in my mind, after all. And I believed that everything else about me – my morals, my sense of right and wrong – was somehow a lie. Why? Because of what I believed about myself. Obviously, I know now that's not true.

CORE BELIEFS

Let's briefly explore the concept of belief for a moment. What is a belief, and have you ever thought about it? That's the thing, beliefs aren't thoughts. You don't think you believe; you know you do. They're powerful emotional attachments to something that you feel you know to be true, and we've been absorbing truths and establishing beliefs since the day we were born. Who, what, where, and when, are safe. Our sense of self. All based on beliefs we've established by absorbing truths. It's pretty much how the socialisation process works. And those early truths are the most important. The core beliefs we establish in early childhood are the building blocks the rest of our life experience is built upon.

We've all heard the phrase that a child's mind is like a sponge, and that's truer than you could imagine. In the early stages of our development – roughly between the ages of two and six – we don't have the ability to analyse or rationalise the information we receive.

Instead, our mind swallows it as a whole, and it becomes truth; our truth. Those early truths then become the essence of who we are, of what we believe about ourselves and, by extension, the world around us. This is the subconscious driving force behind all of our choices and behaviours, yet most of us have no idea. The information was imprinted on to us when we were so young that we weren't even aware of it.

I know there are people out there who think the information we receive as children has no real impact on the choices we make as adults, and that anyone one who says they do is just looking for an excuse. Surely, they say, we've lived long enough and received enough new information to push all the old stuff out of the way and render it obsolete. Funny how those people are usually the same ones who tell you that their upbringing made them who they are.

Aristotle once said, 'Give me a child until he is seven and I'll show you the man.' Even back then, he understood something we still struggle to understand now. By the age of seven we're pretty much emotionally developed and have literally become the man, woman, or anything in between, that we are.

Once our core beliefs have been established, they're unlikely to change, unless of course life takes us to a place where we feel compelled to take a deeper look at ourselves.

The reason they're unlikely to change is because of how strongly we hold onto them, even when they're harmful. We defend them fiercely and train our brain to dismiss, ignore, or disregard any information that might contradict them, no matter how sensible or rational that might be. And at the same time, we hold onto any thought, idea, or information that reinforces that which we've already convinced ourselves to be true.

That cycle of thoughts, feelings, and behaviours reinforcing each other begins to create neuropathways. And the more we revisit the same information and re-enact those cycles, the stronger those pathways become, reinforced by a substance called myelin. To give you something to visualise, imagine the plastic insulation on a copper electrical cable. Every time we wander along those well-trodden pathways, the insulation gets thicker.

The good news, though, is that our brain is an ever-evolving and adaptable machine. Our old, well-trodden paths will never completely go away, but we can create new ones. And the more we walk our new paths, the less maintained the old ones become. Our brain even does some recycling by stripping away the insulation from the old paths and using it to reinforce the new ones.

This all begins to happen when we start to change what we believe about ourselves. This change works two ways. From the outside in, and the inside out.

Even before I got clean, I looked at the world and looked at myself, and saw that there was something very wrong. I claimed I was happy enough, though I clearly wasn't. I used to look out into the world and feel jealous of people doing everyday things. I know that I said that I went to university by accident, but there had always been that underlying urge. A feeling that maybe if I did what other people did, I might find some sense of happiness and fulfilment in my life. And eventually I did.

Over time, what I saw in the outside world sparked something inside me and encouraged me to force myself to start doing things outside my comfort zone. When I discovered those things were safe, I tried more. And it was that initial and very subtle emotional shift that led me to where I am now. Day after day, week after week, month after month, and year after year. Gently nudging yourself out of your comfort zone is a lengthy process. But it's worth it; it's all worth it.

COGNITIVE 'DIS-OWNANCE'

Anyone with any sense doesn't need to read a book written by me – or anyone else for that matter – to know that with change comes obstacles. One of these being the inner struggle that is cognitive dissonance. Or as l call it, cognitive dis-ownance.

The old you doesn't just vanish when the new you appears; they co-exist, with the old one growing quieter and more manageable as time goes on. There may even be parts of your old self which you very much want to keep. I know I did. But the inner struggle happens when the new you meets the parts of the old one that no longer serve you, especially when it comes to your sense of self.

The whole process starts when we have faith in that spark of belief that things could be different, and we begin to think about how to make that difference possible. Cognitive dis-ownance is inner conflict between our old beliefs and the new ones we are in the process of establishing.

There will always be events and interactions in day-to-day life that trigger us and might cause us to meander down the wrong road, to places we no longer wish to visit.

However, the good thing is that now you've discovered alternative routes that are signposted and well lit, so even if you do get lost you can always find your way back. And just like the old pathways, the more you visit the new ones the clearer and more established they become.

Making the transition from unlovable to lovable, and from monstrous to human, was a long road for me. Remember the bubble in my head? All that was cognitive dissonance. The person I believed myself to be, and the person I once hoped to become and was now becoming, battling it out.

But this is a battle you can't lose, unless you give up the fight entirely. It just takes time for your psyche to settle. You'll never be one hundred percent in either direction, though. There will always be some element of darkness, no matter how bright the light becomes. One cannot exist without the other.

I'm happy with a seventy-thirty split in favour of the good guy. And I admit that from time to time I'll walk into a room and convince myself that no-one there likes me… before I've even opened my mouth. The difference now, though, is that this doesn't necessarily have to be true.

THE ITCHY TRIGGER FINGER

It's time to talk about triggers again and, more importantly, how to manage them.

To be triggered is to have an unconditional and sometimes overwhelming emotional response to some kind of stimulus, which stems from our own personal life experience.

People, places, sounds, smells, words, and our own memories can all set off an unconditional emotional response, diverting us back to one of those old unused roads we have worked so hard to leave behind.

When those emotional memories are awakened, they often wake up all the other thoughts and feelings we associate with them. For instance, you might be having an argument with your partner, and they suddenly start to bring up events from months or even years before. The argument has woken up all those emotional memories they had stored away, and they're not just angry about what you've done now but about everything you've ever done.

An inability to understand and manage triggers can be debilitating, but that's where our self-management tools and tactics step in to help us out. And it's where I found that practices like yoga and meditation really worked for me. I accept that you're not going to go into downward facing dog standing at the bus stop because your head is full of broken bottles, but the idea is to apply off the mat what you've learned on the mat.

You can balance your knees on your elbows and take pictures for Instagram all you want, but if you can't apply that yogic mindset to real-life situations, you were never really doing yoga in the first place.

Saying – or in this case even writing – Instagram still sounds weird to me, almost like the kind of thing you save your dealer's number under in your phone. But I was an addict for over twenty years, so my brain most likely interprets things in ways that most other people's brains won't.

To understand what I really mean, we have to move away from the modern pseudo-spirituality which most people associate with yoga, and instead look at it as a stress management tool that helps us learn to regulate our emotions.

Anyone who has ever practised yoga can tell you that intense practice can be a bit of an emotional rollercoaster, especially if you've already been doing a high lunge for twenty breaths when the teacher stops to adjust someone's posture and forgets about the rest of the class.

Yoga also draws your emotions out of you like a poultice on a wound, then teaches you how to use breath to help you self-regulate. The sense of calm that you feel from yoga, or meditation, really has nothing to do with spirituality; it's basic biology. Although it's fair to say that modern discoveries have shown science and spirituality sometimes go hand-in-hand.

If you've ever wondered why yoga and meditation are so popular among people with addiction issues, it's because diaphragmatic breathing gets you high.

There are three types of breathing. Costal breathing is the kind of breathing you are doing right now without even thinking about it. Coastal breathing is the heavy panting using the upper lungs just underneath the clavicle bones, hence the name. It's the kind of breathing we associate with cardiovascular exercise or intense sex (which are just one and the same if you do them properly). And there's diaromatic breathing, which is the deep breath using the bottom of the lungs incorporating the diaphragm.

For the meditative or yogic breath that I'm suggesting you incorporate into your tools, breathing through the nose is very important. There are blood vessels in the nose which heat up the air on inhalation, causing the denser oxygen-rich air to separate and sink to the blood vessels at the base of the lungs. When we're stressed or anxious, we are tapped into our sympathetic nervous system's fight or flight mode. That's when our emotions are literally telling our brain that some sort of threat is coming, and we might need to fight or run. When our blood is richer in oxygen, though, it gives our rational brain more fuel to better analyse the threat.

And taking the time to breathe allows us to pause and gain perspective and see that what we told our brain was a threat wasn't a threat at all. Diaphragmatic breathing also stimulates the Vagas nerve, which lets us tap out of our sympathetic nervous system and into our parasympathetic nervous system. And that's what really brings that sense of calm after a yoga class or a guided meditation.

Something else I've found works really well, and might work for you, is the SMART recovery hierarchy of values. Self-Management And Recovery Training (SMART) is a self-help approach where groups are led by trained facilitators using a variety of CBT (Cognitive Behavioural Therapy) tools and techniques to help them manage problematic behaviours. Ok, so this one was specifically created to work with people who have addiction issues, but you can apply it to any decision-making process.

The hierarchy of values is a visual tool that not only aids the decision-making process but also helps when we've been triggered or have the urge to do something we know we shouldn't. As you can imagine, when an addict gets triggered, it usually involves using substances, but you could apply this to any situation. You hold your hand out in front of you and imagine that the choice or decision is in the centre of your palm, and that each finger represents how that choice will affect your life.

This works well with the mindful or diaphragmatic breathing, taking the time to pause and letting the breath do its job, then looking at your hand and visualising what the potential outcomes of your decision could be.

Personally, this worked for me on several occasions where the 'disease ideology' would have let me down. Again, I'm not bashing fellowships; I'm just being honest. When you believe that your decisions are at least partly controlled by a disease that can render you powerless, and that the disease is chronic and incurable, there is always a chance that the disease could win. That leaves us with the question: were we really overpowered by our disease, or did we use the idea of rendering us powerless to justify a poor life choice? No-one really knows, and most with personal experience of this might not be honest about it, even with themselves.

With the hierarchy of values, the decision is all yours. Even if you do think addiction is a disease, it gives you the choice to recognise that you've been triggered and either walk away or call your sponsor and talk it through. You become empowered instead of being powerless. You start to become your own higher power.

I know this works, because I've done it. And you might remember when I said this helped me when the fellowship approach might have let me down.

When I was around the four-year mark of being clean, my brother and his girlfriend at the time thought it would be a nice idea if both families went away to spend New Year together. So, a whole crowd of us rented a cottage on a farm out in Dumfries – me, my mum, my brother and his kids, his girlfriend and her kids, and her friend with her daughter.

On New Year's Eve, shortly after the bells, my mum and all the kids went to bed. And the two couples (which is the way things turned out... for a few weeks at least) decided to fire up the hot tub.

It was picturesque. We were in the hot tub, it was snowing, the girls were in bikinis drinking martinis– real *Wolf of Wall Street* kings for a day kinda shit. My brother and I were in and out of the cottage mixing drinks, while we stuck to the alcohol-free wine.

At one point I was in the kitchen alone, and there was a bottle of Grey Goose vodka sitting on the table. And there it was… that soft little whisper. *'You know what would make our night better? Drinking that vodka. Just drink it, no-one would even know.'*

It wasn't just a thought; it was an urge. I was so caught up in the moment I wanted to drink it.

If I believed that addiction was a disease that I was powerless over and that could never be fully cured, it would have been easy for me to say on that day that I lost the battle and the disease won.

Instead, I held my hand out, thought about the choices and the consequences each choice might have. And I remembered that I was only in that moment because I wasn't using in the first place. It was a trade-off. You can have all this, or you can have what's in that bottle.

So, I made my choice, and for the second time in my life I left the bottle where it was and chose a different path.

HIDDEN TRAUMA

Sometimes when we're in the process of closing certain doors, we open other doors we didn't even know were there. Memories which had been long buried start bubbling up to the surface. At first, I wasn't even sure if what I remembered was real or something I had dreamt. But the more I spoke about it, the more vivid the memory became.

That's the thing about trauma. People think if the event was really significant you couldn't possibly forget it. But as we know, the brain is a cleverly constructed piece of kit, and it's been programmed to keep us safe. That's why it sometimes pushes hurtful memories so far down that we forget all about them. And they sit buried in our subconscious, just like our core beliefs, affecting our lives in ways we don't even realise.

The things I was remembering were very real, although they hadn't happened to me directly. It was something I saw as a child that changed who I was and how I viewed the world before I was old enough to even understand what I saw.

I was only young – maybe four, at most – and it must have been the weekend, because my mum was taking my brother and me to the park. Every weekend we would go there with a picnic, feed the ducks, play on the swings, and go to the koi pond in the glasshouse at the top of the hill to feed the fish with Wotsits.

My brother was still being pushed in the pram while I was walking beside her like a big boy. I probably shouldn't be making jokes, but this is something that I've worked through, and adding a bit humour while I talk about it reminds me that I'm the one in charge.

We were going to the park on what happened to be the day of Glasgow's big annual orange walk. There are two subjects people in Glasgow take a little more seriously than they should, and that's football and religion. And to some people, the two are pretty much indivisible.

I don't know why, but one of the guys from the walk must have gotten a bit carried away, and for some reason he decided to go into an Irish pub in a predominantly Catholic area while singing Protestant songs and wearing his orange sash.

As our happy little family unit was walking along, suddenly there was a tussle in the doorway. One of the guys from the pub had taken offence and glassed the guy wearing the sash in the throat.

Obviously, I didn't understand all the details back then, but all I knew was my mum trying to drag me away, while the guy who had been glassed was lying slumped on the ground with blood pumping out of his neck. There were two women screaming for help while they used bar towels to try and stop the bleeding.

I'm clearly writing this now as an adult who can make more sense of the details than the child that witnessed them. And it's not that I didn't remember it; it's just that it didn't seem real, more like something in a film.

How I remembered it doesn't really matter now, but what matters is that this was a defining moment in my life. Yet I had no idea how significant it was until I finally started to piece things together, and it all made sense.

One of the things everyone had struggled to understand – including me – was why I was so reluctant to defend myself when I was being bullied at school, even when I was being subjected to emotional and physical abuse on a daily basis. But now I understand that witnessing such a horrific event at such a young age left with me an aversion to violence. The idea of any kind of physical confrontation made me feel uncomfortable for a very long time, so I was reluctant to stand up for myself. Unfortunately, that made me an easy target, and the bullying got worse.

When life became unbearable, I started looking for things I could use to change how I felt, and the cycle of addiction began. Food, porn, self-harm, drugs; they were all just negative coping strategies that I developed in childhood.

Finally, I could make sense of how it started and where my addictive behaviours had come from. The next question, though, was why. There were people in the world who had been through similar experiences, or worse. I know everything is subjective, and there's no grading system for how traumatised someone is by their experiences, but there's no denying some stories are more horrific than others. Yet some of these people never turned to drugs or alcohol to help them cope.

What I found even more intriguing was why people seemed to process and recall similar experiences so differently. For example, how could two siblings of similar ages grow up in the same house, with the same parents, in the same area, yet have completely different recollections of their childhood? And why does one grow up to be an addict while the other one doesn't? Was there really some genetic predisposition I didn't understand? And if so, what caused it? There had to be a reason.

FILLING THE VOID

If you've read this far in the book and still think drug addicts are lazy, then you either weren't paying attention or you hold that belief so strongly that you can't be convinced otherwise. Self-indulgent maybe, but definitely not lazy. We really are quite an industrious group and would go to almost any length to get our next fix. And that's why so many drug users go on to be such productive members of society after they get clean.

We're some of the most determined and hardworking people on the planet, given the right kind of motivation. Our problem is that we simply chose to channel all that energy into the wrong things. Then again, that's because most of us were trying to shield ourselves from a life or a world in which we essentially felt victimised. So, the only parts that were really wrong were how our choices affected other people.

All that deceit, the lying, the grafting, running about trying to score, and in most cases trying our best to at least hide the extent of our using from the people in our lives – it all takes a lot of effort. Believe me, it's a highly energetic and very stressful lifestyle.

That chaotic energy is what's known as the addictive drive. And sometimes, as stressful and destructive as being an addict may be, it can be very exciting, particularly compared to working a regular 9 to 5.

When we put the drugs down, though, all that energy has nowhere to go. It creates a void, a vacuum, an empty space in our lives where all that chaos used to be. And it doesn't take long before we start to feel lifeless, our new world becomes boring, and we begin to crave something that stimulates us beyond the mundane.

The best thing we can do in that situation is to replace all those old behaviours with new ones as quickly as possible.

I was lucky, because I had someone to help me right from the off. My brother showed me all the things that had worked for him when he got clean, and some of those things worked for me while others didn't. But the point is that I started replacing old behaviours with new ones pretty much straight away. And my brother's enthusiasm meant that sometimes I didn't really have much choice. I know I moaned about that at the time, but now I'm very grateful because his enthusiasm was one of the foundation stones that the rest of my road was built upon.

If you do find yourself unfortunate enough to be going through this alone, with no-one to go with you and encourage you to try new things, don't worry. It might not feel like it, but you're in a fantastic position. Getting clean is a voyage of self-discovery, a chance for you to finally start to figure out who you are, and maybe even what you might be capable of.

I know the very idea of trying things on your own can be terrifying, because your head is full of what ifs and maybes – and not the good kind either. You walk into a room full of strangers and you feel like everyone is staring at you because you don't belong. Your tongue seems to swell in your mouth, and you lose the ability to form words and sentences. You're convinced everyone else thinks you're a prick, when really they're only wondering who the new person is.

And even if they do think you're a prick or try and make you feel like you don't belong there… fuck them! You've got just as much right to be there and enjoy your life as anyone else.

Don't listen to those negative thoughts either. The ones that tell you you're no good and not capable – you just have to push through those. I've got a voice that tells me I'm not capable of things all the time, even while I'm doing them. Even now, as I sit here writing this book, I have thoughts telling me that my writing is shit, I'm not intelligent enough to write a book, and that no-one will read it. But if you're sitting there with this book in your hand, it shows you that some of my thoughts are wrong. And that means some of yours are probably wrong, too.

When I first got clean, I threw myself into every new and positive behaviour and opportunity that was presented to me. Voluntary work, yoga practice, decorating my new flat, martial arts, exercise, education, new training opportunities. I was more productive during my first two years clean than I had been for most of my life. I felt like I had been given another shot, a second chance.

Within six months of getting clean I was a practising holistic therapist; by eighteen months I had completed the 12-Step programme. Then just two years after getting clean I went on to study counselling.

And that enthusiasm for life has never left me.

THE WOLF AND THE CHILD

It was during my own voyage of self-discovery that I found out how complex human beings actually are, and how fragmented we can sometimes be. There are many selves within the self that all need acceptance and healing.

I found that hiding in me there was a shadow monster, a vulnerable child, and a parent that could either be enablingly nurturing or overbearingly critical depending on the situation and where I was emotionally. These are all entities that I have come to know and accept. I've even had the privilege of meeting the child and the shadow face-to-face.

These are the voices in our head, the ones that tell us that the world is harsh and unfair, or when we've done well and should be proud, or when we're worthless and aren't enough. And of course, there's the one that whispers the disturbing things that we think in our head but would most likely never say out loud.

Now, I'm pretty sure I know the first thing on your mind is that either sounds interesting or this guy's full of shit. Either way, I came to meet all these different parts of me through yoga, meditation, and shamanic practice.

It seems to be commonplace now, in the spiritually well community, that people use ayahuasca, psilocybin, or kambo – dried secretion of poisonous frogs – to embark on journeys of spiritual and emotional healing. These are all well-established treatments in indigenous cultures around the world. And I'm not saying you shouldn't do these things, but I am suggesting you try to see how far you can get with simple breathwork first, as you'll be astounded at how effective it is.

I realise there is a chance that my years of drug use have opened doors in my mind that other people might find inaccessible. But meditation, if done correctly, will get you high and place your mind into such a relaxed state that it allows you to tap into your subconscious – where these hidden parts of self have a tendency to make themselves known. And sometimes your breath can take you there without you even trying.

My shadow was the first to reveal itself to me. I say reveal itself, but really it was an image my mind had created, based on my own knowledge, experience, and belief system, symbolising the part of my psyche I was dealing with at the time. This happened while I was on my counselling course, coming to terms with my Inner Viking – the part of me that I used to justify the belief that I was monstrous and unlovable.

I was attending a workshop on yin yoga – a technique I had taken to practising with my eyes shut, like a gentle form of sensory deprivation. I could still hear everything, but my mind was free to wander into the darkness, showing me what it felt I needed to see.

Yin yoga mostly takes place on the floor, so you don't have to worry about falling, and once you've been practising it for a while you don't really need to watch the teacher all that much; listening is enough. Yin yoga had become my safe place where I could explore my emotions and make myself vulnerable, and I'm not ashamed to say that I shed tears more than once on the mat.

On that occasion, I was taking part in a four-hour yin yoga workshop, going through what was already a massive internal emotional process.

I was in a posture called dragon, which doesn't sound too peaceful – because it's not. This is a very challenging low lunge that's usually held for a minimum of three minutes, which is enough to make anyone feel vulnerable.

I'd had my eyes shut for most of the practice, and it felt as if I was just floating in my own space. Then there it was. Through the dancing colours and time travelling stars came a big black werewolf. He was colossal, muscular, like a demon from some Japanese cartoon. I didn't even have to guess; I knew exactly who he was. And it didn't take long for me to figure out why I had manifested his image as a wolf either.

As I had been going through the programme, my sponsor had related the Navaho tale of the two wolves. The story goes that inside of all of us there are two wolves: one black, one white, each feeding on our emotional experiences. The black wolf feeds on our anger, fear, and inadequacies, and all the negative parts of self; the white wolf feeds on love, happiness, and positivity. Both wolves have the power to consume and devour us. The question is which wolf you are going to feed.

I had subconsciously taken that image and used it to create the monster that represented my dark half, which was what my mind was suddenly showing me. The monster that represented all of my rage, hurt, insecurities, and darker urges. All the parts of me that I struggled to accept.

I found the inner child, however, a little more difficult to figure out. I met him in a crystal healing workshop led by my first reiki teacher Linda Thomson at her flat in Maryhill. She was leading us through a meditation that would let us meet a part of ourselves that was hidden. We were to visualise ourselves sitting on a bench in the middle of a field with a large boulder next to it. Then the part of us that was hiding would come out from behind the boulder and show itself to us.

In that moment, I wasn't exactly sure what I saw. It was a small creature that I can only describe as a combination of Dobby the house elf and Tommy Pickles from the Rugrats, which came out from behind the boulder, dressed in rags. He sat next to me on the bench and looked up at me with huge black tearful eyes and told me that he was lonely. Then he just disappeared.

Afterwards, I spoke about it with the group, and Linda was the one who suggested that what I had seen was my inner child because of the way I had described it. But I couldn't understand why he had looked like that. The whole thing freaked me out a bit, leaving me feeling a bit shaken and unsettled.

I discussed it with my sponsor and a few chosen others, including my friend Katey. Katey had once been an addiction worker, and we met through my brother and got to know each other through our yoga practice. She was, at the time, a shamanic practitioner. I know it all sounds a bit out there, but these people exist if you look in the right places or, like most things, they come to you when you need them in ways you don't expect.

Together we all made it make sense. That part of me had been locked away in a dark room in my mind, starved and unattended for a very long time. Now it was time for him to step back out into the world again.

THE MERGING OF MAN AND BOY

I'm not going to say that the reintegration of the shadow self is easy, but it was a lot more straightforward than getting to know my inner child. It's always easier to work with something when you're already familiar with it, but up until I met him, I had no idea that my inner child even existed. If I wanted the chance to become reacquainted, though, I was going to have to find him.

The first question I had was whether that really was my inner child I saw, and why he looked like that. Why didn't he just look like a childhood me?

After some long and very emotional conversations with my sponsor and Katey, we finally came up with that answer. The part of my psyche that was my inner child had been locked away in a room on his own, starved and neglected, for decades. So, it was only understandable that he would be so unrecognisable. The poor little guy had never had the chance to grow with the rest of me, leaving him twisted and malnourished.

Now that I knew about him, my next challenge was how I could bring him back.

There are lots of different methods for reintegrating your inner child into your psyche. Standing in front of a mirror and speaking to them directly; or writing them a letter, then using your non-dominant hand to allow your inner child to write a response. However, I had a shaman in my corner, so I decided to do something called a shamanic soul retrieval. This is where the shaman uses breathwork to put you into a meditative state, then goes into your psychic plane to find whatever part of you has been splintered off, and bring it back.

No, you've not accidentally stumbled into a Hogwarts class.

This is actually a form of disassociation. Sometimes, when people experience some type of trauma or systematic abuse, the part of us which experiences those things becomes trapped there. And there are millions of people out there with a fragmented psyche contributing to any manner of mental and emotional health issues. Just like with our core beliefs, in many cases they are probably not even aware of it.

In my case, this was the part of me that had decided to hide away because the world wasn't safe for him. Well, now it was time to bring him back.

My friend Katey and I went for lunch to discuss the ritual and what it would involve. As we were speaking, I saw her looking past me, over my shoulder. I asked if she had seen someone she knew, but she said the little guy we were trying to find was standing behind my left shoulder. Whether she could see him or not is a question I couldn't possibly answer. But she did find him, so maybe she did.

For the ritual, I had to go to Katey's house, which she had turned into her very own shamanic grotto, with incense burning, and skulls and feathers lying around. It reminded me of my own house.

Just like any other ritual, there are stages to shamanic healing, and my first stage was the talking stone. This is when you set your intention. Katey asked me to put my hand on a large, flat piece of slate stone and basically vent. She told me to verbally let out all of my trauma and how it made me feel.

By the time I was finished, I was sweating, and the stone was warm to the touch, as if it had absorbed everything I'd said and taken it from me.

Then it was time for the real work, the breathwork. Katey made me lie down blindfolded and she applied acupuncture needles to the Shen men point in my ears. Then the drumming started, with the odd bit of chanting here and there, too. There's something about the rhythmic beat of shamanic drumming that takes to me places other forms of meditation and sound healing just can't seem to reach.

My body might have been grounded in Katey's flat that day, but in my mind I was flying over trees silhouetted against a purple sky, before swooping down into a cave and swimming through an underground river. Apparently, I was experiencing something known as the piercing of the veil. They say this is when you enter the spirit realm, but I see it more as accessing the subconscious mind and everything that comes along with it.

At that point Katey told me to start taking deep breaths, and she pushed down hard on my diaphragm on the exhale, forcing all the air out of my body. This was to release whatever experiences I was ready to let go. Then the drumming started again, only much faster, and with Katey chanting this time.

And that's when I felt it. It was as if something latched onto my right-hand side and was absorbed by my body. And just like that, my inner child was released and brought back to me. But it gave me a responsibility. I wasn't just the child; I was both the child and the parent.

That takes me back to that conversation about putting the tree up at Christmas. Wee Tony might not have been a physical child, but he was a very real child in the psychological and emotional sense. And after all those years locked in the cupboard in my head, I think his needs were more important than anyone else's.

ACCEPTANCE AND REINTEGRATION

Reintegrating the parts of yourself that were once lost, or that you had denied the existence of altogether – for whatever reason – isn't as difficult as you might think. And just like getting clean, it all begins with acceptance. You have to start off by accepting that these parts of you exist, and in most cases they're nothing to be ashamed of. There's a murderous werewolf and a vulnerable chid in all of us, and just like every other part of us they only want to be accepted for what they are. They just want to be, well, part of us. The real suffering only comes when we try to exclude them, because that's what leads to the internal conflict.

I had found it easier to reintegrate my shadow, simply because he wasn't hidden. He had always been there, challenging my morals, making me question my sanity, the very nature of who I was, with his whispers of violence and debauchery.

I had already established the belief that I was in some way monstrous because I felt shunned and excluded by the world. And I'd used those unwanted thoughts to reinforce that belief. I really was the monster I believed myself to be; I must have been. The truth was that I was just trying to make sense of why the world would treat me the way it did, so I had convinced myself that there must be something fundamentally wrong with me.

When I finally spoke about all this after holding it for so long, I learned to get comfortable with it. Then, like I said, I started paying more attention to the world around me: music, films, stand-up comedians, even the things my friends said. People hadn't just accepted the darker part of themselves and made peace with it; they were using it as inspiration for jokes and other forms of artistic expression. They had made it part of them, so there was no reason why mine couldn't be part of me.

That realisation completely redefined how I felt about myself, and I no longer saw myself as a monster. I was a good, well-balanced human with strong morals who just didn't know how to understand himself. Think about it: if I found the mere thought of something so disturbing that it could make me have a panic attack, there's no way I could ever act that thought out.

There are, however, some situations where you express or even indulge the shadier half of yourself.

I'm of the opinion that almost any scenario can be acted out between two consenting adults. You can live your life any way you like, as long as you can do it without intentionally hurting someone else – unless, of course, that's also consensual. Sexual fantasies, no matter how seemingly depraved, can be acted out between two loving and accepting partners. In fact, speaking from experience, relationships in which people are not only allowed, but encouraged, to share and act out their fantasies can offer a deeper level of emotional connection.

It's easy to show your partner the part of you that you show to the rest of the world, but showing them what lies beneath takes a lot of trust. Yet showing someone your shadow can offer a level of closeness and intimacy that some people unfortunately never get to experience.

Even our more violent urges can be indulged once we have accepted that they're part of us. On the more extreme end of the spectrum, there are football groups of hooligans throughout Europe who meet in secluded forests and fields far away from the rest of the public, battling it out like gladiators.

Obviously, I'm not suggesting you put on a gumshield and go out into the woods and beat the shit out of each other. I found that some style of martial arts practice, or aggressive contact sport, was enough for me. And over the years I've practised Muay Thai boxing, Kung-fu, Aikido, and Iaidio – a form of Japanese sword work. I have also tried historical European martial arts, such as broadsword and sabre, though I much prefer archery to fencing. I mean, why go toe-to-toe when you could just take someone out from a distance? Hypothetically, of course.

My point is that there are many ways to indulge the more savage part of your nature without hurting anyone, including yourself.

And now I've recently discovered that stand-up comedy is a fantastic medium for not only venting my underlying madness, but also reclaiming my power from thoughts, feelings, and situations that once made me feel anxious and uncomfortable. I've even managed to figure out why comedy makes people feel better, and why the more outlandish comedians are usually the most popular.

Yes, they make us laugh, but it's deeper than that. When a comedian openly unleashes their madness, it makes us feel better about our own. We see someone that's so self-accepting that they're willing to make themselves vulnerable by verbalising their inner monologue to a room full of strangers. Seeing them do that makes us feel more comfortable within ourselves and helps us to see that no matter how fucked-up our thoughts are, they're only thoughts and don't have to be taken seriously.

THE UNDERLYING CAUSE

Everything I had learned about addiction from counselling and psychology made sense to me. It made sense that negative experiences would lead to negative beliefs. And that, in turn, those beliefs would lead to more negative experiences as well as harmful, destructive behaviours. What I didn't get was why some people who had negative experiences became addicts while others didn't. Was there really some underlying genetic predisposition I didn't know about, or just didn't understand? And if there was, how could such a thing be possible? If we were born defective, there must be a cause... right?

My path had taken me down a lot of different roads, and I was lucky enough to learn from the people who took the time to teach me things. One of those things was traditional Chinese Medicine, though not the tea brewing, or potion making. You might be disappointed to hear that I can't cure impotence by mixing powdered rhino horn with some dehydrated tiger penis. Although, after learning about some aspects of Chinese medicine, me and two friends did decide to drink our own urine for a month. And I'll be honest, I am not a fan! It won't cleanse your body or detox your liver, but it will treat gum infection. I've tried it, and my advice is: Don't do it.

Drinking my own pish wasn't the only research I did, though, as I also read some books and watched lectures. The concept in traditional Chinese medicine that I found fascinating was something known as Jing Qi Shen. Jing means seed, or essence; Qi means life force, or even breath; and Shen means soul, or supernatural being. And they are the first three treasures on the path of Dao (Daoism/Taoism – a system of Chinese philosophy based on the writings of Lao-tzu). Jing, Qi, and Shen are the essential components for conscious life, with consciousness present in every cell.

In Chinese medicine it is believed that our cells aren't just conscious but have their own emotional memory. And memories and emotional experiences can be passed down inherently from generation to generation. The Chinese say that there is a point – approximately five or six vertebrae up from the base of the spine – which is known as the Jin Qi Jing Qi point, or the spark of life, and this is where the cells start to merge together. And, as theory goes, that spark also carries the emotional memories and imprinted experiences of all the generations before us, now fused into the cells of our body.

If that is true, it could explain inherent generational trauma. But how could anything like that even be possible?

THE EMOTIONAL MEMORY OF WATER

My seemingly endless quest for answers led me from China to Japan – though not physically, of course. I mean I took my Google search history and my Amazon book purchases from China to Japan. I discovered there was a Japanese scientist by the name of Dr Masaru Emoto – an uncanny name for man in his field of study – who was looking into the emotional memory of water, particularly how negative emotions might contribute to the growth of cancer cells.

ND Emoto took three sample bottles of water from the same source. He labelled one bottle 'love', another one 'hate', and the third he left unlabelled as a control sample. He then treated each bottle in accordance with its label. He told the bottle marked 'love' that it was loved and appreciated, and he played it classical music and so on. He told the bottle marked 'hate' that he despised it, that it was worthless, and played it 'angry' or aggressive music. And he left the control bottle untouched so that it remained neutral.

As a long-term heavy metal fan and proud listener of what is often referred to as 'angry music', I'm not fully convinced about that part. However, the experiment did yield some interesting results. He found that each bottle had a different pH level, and that in each one the water's structure crystallised in different forms under a microscope.

The water that was loved had a more alkaline pH balance, whereas the one that was hated was more acidic. And there have been studies which claim that cancer cells grow more quickly in an acidic environment, though this is something I've spent a lot of time looking into myself.

Ok, so some crazy Japanese scientist claimed that he changed the pH of water by shouting at it. Even if it were true, it doesn't prove anything. And while this one experiment would be easy to dismiss on its own, there have been other studies with similar results.

The Aerospace Institute in Stuttgart conducted an experiment in which a room full of people was asked to take a syringe and draw water from the same source, then create a series of water droplets. By examining the water under a microscope, they found that each person produced a different and distinct water droplet from other people, although each person's own water droplets were the same. They were also all different to the control samples of water from the same source.

So, what does any of this prove, and why is water even relevant in the first place? Because about sixty percent of the human body is water at a cellular level. And, in the most basic of terms, at the point of conception we are made from the donor cells of both our parents. If we are sixty percent water, and water has the ability to retain some kind of emotional memory, it would be entirely possible for positive – or negative – emotions to be trapped inside the body and transferred to our children at the point of conception. This meant generational trauma wasn't just behavioural; it was imprinted into our DNA.

Could this be it? Had I cracked it? Was this the key to genetic predisposition, or inherent trauma? Was it possible for people to be pre-charged with negative emotions, held deep inside the very building blocks of their body?

If so, it not only explained everything, but it meant that both nature and nurture played as big a part as each other. Generation after generation of unresolved emotion secretly steering our lives, fused into our very core.

If that was the case, how many generations of emotion were we carrying? And was it something we could ever really heal from?

BETTER THAN WELL

So, if everything we do is governed by beliefs that we've established in early childhood because of our own life experiences, which in turn were pre-determined by an inherent predisposition to negativity, was this something we could ever heal from? Was it possible for people like me to ever get better?

There is a widespread phenomenon in the field of 'recovery' from addiction: The 'better than well' principle. It's the idea that after five years without using, and doing the right kind of emotional work, someone in 'recovery' can sometimes be more motivated and contribute more to society than people who have never had any issues with addiction.

Obviously personal success depends on the individual. But on average I would say that a person who had managed to rebuild themselves after a life of addiction would be more grateful for the new life that they've been given. I know I am, despite its challenges. And the more grateful a person is, the more productive they're likely to be.

While this kind of change in someone is extremely visible, there's another bigger – and I believe even more significant – transformation taking place. Over the course of seven years, the cells in our body are completely renewed. So, if the cells in our body really do have the kind of emotional memory that I've previously described – and I believe they do – this would account for another type of phenomenon: the seven-year cycle of change. This is believed to not only be a process of self-development and self-understanding but also of emotional and spiritual evolution.

The first three seven-year segments of our lives – 0 to 7; 7 to 14; and 14 to 21 – see us transition from childhood, through to puberty, and then into adulthood. At this point I'll remind you again of Aristotle's famous quote: 'Show me a child of seven and I'll show you a man.' Maybe back then Aristotle had this figured in a way we still struggle to understand even now. During the rest of these cycles, we start to question who we are, why we're here, and what our purpose is.

I can even relate this idea to how I changed and developed over the course of my own life. I was comfort eating by the time I was seven, discovered drugs at fourteen, relapsed at twenty-one, lost a landscaping business to cocaine addiction when I was twenty-eight, then finally got clean just as I was about to turn thirty-five. And there is one more significant life event… but you'll have to wait till the next chapter for that.

So even my own life tells me that there's something to this, even if it seems out there and far-fetched to some of you.

However, here's where it gets a bit more complicated. If the inherent emotional content of our cells was a governing force in our emotional response to life, which then led us into a self-perpetuating cycle of negative feeling and experiences, but those cells were replaced with new ones every seven years… that predetermining factor would become irrelevant. We would be fully responsible for the emotional content of our cells, because all our inherent pre-programming had been filtered out.

I know, I know. But as whacky as all of this sounds, I still say that it makes more sense than a disease that no-one can explain or the idea that we're one of God's chosen few. And it offers more hope, too. Old-school thinking tells you that no matter what you do or how hard you work, you will always be an addict that's recovering from a disease that you can never fully recover from. It stays with you for life. But not anymore.

With this kind of thinking, it is possible – not just for addicts, but for everyone – to free themselves from anything, including the inherent emotional programming that shackled us to lives that made us unhappy.

THE NEXT SEVEN-YEAR CYCLE

I had it sussed. I had answers to all the unanswerable questions that finally made sense to me. There was only one problem: I didn't feel any different. Not really. Yeah, my life was better, and I was in a much better place, and there was no denying that I had worked through a lot of my issues and started to figure out who, and why, I was.

But I didn't feel different, not on the inside. I didn't feel comfortable within myself or around other people, especially other men. And it still felt as if my brain wasn't quite together. It was as though I was in two separate pieces that never met in the middle the way they were supposed to.

I couldn't understand it. I had done all the work – more work than most – yet I still just didn't feel right. And when I tried to explain it to other people, you can guess what their answer was. They referred to the 'disease of addiction' as if it could be used as a blanket term of any and all forms of emotional or psychological discomfort.

Yet I knew why I had used, or at least I thought I did. And this feeling of discomfort had nothing to do with my drug use or the contributing emotional factors behind it; this was something different entirely, and I thought I would just have to live with it without ever knowing what it was.

And then it came. At seven years' clean, I came to the end of another seven-year cycle.

It all started at the beginning of 2022. I was off work with what I then believed to be seasonal depression. Much like everyone else, my mental health had suffered during the great Covid-19 saga, and my resilience had been lowered so much that even the ghosts of the past I had already made peace with were coming back to haunt me.

I was having vivid flashbacks of the most terrible things I had done. My thoughts of suicide had never left me; they had just become quieter. And now my head was convincing me I didn't deserve to live again.

I'm a lot of things, but silly isn't one of them. I understood what this meant. It was time to strip away another layer from the onion. I wasn't having flashbacks about things that had happened to me; I was having them about things I had done to other people… which is worse. This time I didn't have the comfort of being the victim; in this part of the story, I was very much the monster I had once believed myself to be.

I couldn't love myself, which meant the child inside me that I had spent so much time nurturing was once again being neglected.

While all this was going on, I found comfort in a partner – a girl that I loved and adored enough to distract myself from my internal struggle. But I knew there was some part of me I had to make peace with. I wasn't the bad guy anymore, so I had to let him go.

I went back to see my friend Katey, the shaman who had helped me reconnect with wee Tony and brought him back to me. Katey didn't work like most people, but what more would you expect from a shaman living in the south side of Glasgow? She didn't work for money; all she asked was that I bring her a stick for some unknown purpose. Random, I know, but we're talking about shamanic healing in the Gorbals, and that's about as random as it gets.

This stick, which I found in the park on the way to Katey's house, was to be my implement of release. It was to be my talking stick, similar in purpose to the talking stone. I held it in my hand like an antenna and used it to unleash my thoughts and emotions out into the universe. Afterwards, I was so burnt out that I couldn't remember the treatment itself, only being woken up with a cup of warm cocoa. But over the next week or so I began to feel less pulled apart and more or less put together.

Just as I was starting to feel whole again, I realised that I had fallen in love with someone I didn't really know, and that we were both trying to convince each other to be people we weren't. I knew one of us had to be the adult and say it wasn't working, and unfortunately that had to be me. I assure you I was not happy about that, but we were making each other miserable.

It had been an emotional few months, and although the flashbacks had stopped, I was still depressed for reasons I couldn't understand. Then, through the ever-informative medium that is social media, I saw other guys talking about their hormone levels.

In the swamp of drugs and emotions I had been living in, that was something else from my past I had forgotten all about.

My hormone levels had been a concern when I first started puberty. My mum took me to the doctors when I was about eleven (I think), because she felt I wasn't developing properly, and I seemed to be growing breast tissue. This is what we now know as gynecomastia, but none of that was spoken about in 1991, so the doctor just dismissed it and said I was just a late developer.

The issue wasn't mentioned again until I was in my twenties. I had just come off heroin at that time and decided I was going to get my life together.

While I was clean, I saw a TV documentary about the male menopause, with men speaking about how having a low testosterone count was affecting them. So much of what they said sounded very familiar, even though I was less than half the age of even the youngest of them.

So, it was back to the doctor – only this time I could articulate how I felt as an adult. I told her that I didn't feel right within my body, and that it felt like my brain had never quite merged; it was as if there was more than one of me in there. I was also very honest about my drug use.

This time, the doctor didn't just dismiss me. Instead, she tried to tell me I was schizophrenic, which I can assure I am not. Long-term psychotic, yes; schizophrenic, definitely not. At least, I didn't think so.

Shortly after seeing her, I went back on the drugs and the hormonal issue wasn't spoken about again until I was forty-two.

By that stage I had been off the drugs for years and done more internal work than most, yet everyone else had seemed to find a level of happiness and self-acceptance that was unattainable for me. I still didn't feel comfortable within myself, and I thought about suicide all the time. These were symptoms of low testosterone, so I ordered a home testing kit, as I suspected my levels were low.

I found out that I had less testosterone in my system than most eighty-year-old men!

I took the results to another doctor who was less dismissive, and when I explained the history, he referred me to an endocrinology consultant. After four months of blood tests and suicidal ideation, I was finally diagnosed with a condition known as hypogonadism, or underactive testicles. Basically, my balls don't work, my body doesn't make enough male hormones, and I can't make babies.

And that's not even the interesting part.

SEROTONIN AND DOPAMINE

And again, why is this relevant? What could someone's balls not working properly have to do with addiction? Well... men with testosterone deficiency often struggle with chronic depression and suicidal ideation. And they can be more susceptible to addictive behaviours, specifically opiate use. This is because testosterone is at least partly responsible for the production and regulation of other hormones – two of these being dopamine and serotonin, the chemicals in our brain that allow us to feel the sensations of happiness, joy, and satisfaction.

My own experience tells me this all makes sense, because ever since the day I got clean I had missed two substances more than any others – heroin and MDMA (methylenedioxymethamphetamine), also known as Molly, or Mandy, which is the main ingredient in ecstasy. Very specific, I know. But just like everything else, the reason why I missed these two drugs so much was due to the chemicals they release into the brain.

And before I go on, I've discussed everything I'm about to say with two endocrinology consultants. Both men oversee my hormone treatment and monitor my bloods at Stobhill Hospital here in Glasgow, and they both agree that this all makes sense.

Heroin floods dopamine into the brain, and MDMA floods the brain with serotonin – the same two chemicals I was lacking due to a hormone imbalance I didn't even know I had. Unbeknown to me, these two drugs could temporarily relieve my depression by giving my body chemicals it needed but struggled to produce. So, there were at least some points when I was literally self-medicating without realising it.

Am I saying that having a hormone imbalance justifies my using drugs or the other behaviours that went with it? Absolutely not. But it does bring my capability for rational thinking into question. Aside from causing chronic depression, hypogonadism also causes chronic fatigue and impaired cognitive function.

Learning all this made me question everything around my drug use and the choices I had made my whole life. I had been living with chronic depression and brain fog since the beginning of puberty and thought it was normal. I thought everyone else was just like me, but they had somehow managed to learn how to handle life better than I did. But the truth was that I was facing challenges I didn't even know about and was handling them better than most other people would.

All my anger, my rage, my frustration. Was that me trying to act like a man because I didn't feel like one, and because all the examples I had led me to believe that was how men were supposed to act? Did all this put me somewhere on the trans spectrum? I was a man who identified as a man, but I didn't have the hormones I needed to make me a man.

It was all so confusing, and in the midst of all that confusion there were answers. Not just about my using or my behaviour, but about me as a person. I had always felt uncomfortable within myself, around other people, and especially around other men. It was as if I didn't understand them or know how to act around them. I had always been the awkward one who seemed to have something to prove. But that usually made everyone else uncomfortable and made me the group clown, the one they all ripped the pish out of. And that had only left me feeling even more insecure.

Just one more self-perpetuating cycle to add to the list.

THE DOPAMINE CYCLE

As you've read, pulling my life back together has been a long, arduous, and complicated process. It would have been easier if I had just said I had a disease and left it at that. But if you made it this far, you know I am not that guy. And I'm glad I'm not. If I was, I wouldn't be where I am now, which is exactly where I am supposed to be.

I suppose it didn't matter which guy I was, as I would have ended up where I was supposed to be anyway. But certainly, the place I'm in would be different if I was that other guy.

In the nine years I've been clean, I've found out a lot and been given a lot of information to process. I have found a lot of my journey overwhelming, but – going back to the philosopher Kierkegaard – now that I'm separated from the happening, I can get to the knowing. Or at least my own sense of understanding.

I don't know why I used; not definitively. Of course, I had lots of excuses disguised as reasons, and a different way to justify my choices. And that's where the real magic is: in the ownership. It's always a choice… whether we want to admit that to ourselves or not.

Over the years I've heard so many tales of relinquished responsibility: I fell in with wrong crowd; I didn't know what I was taking; someone forced me. Even if all of this was true – and sadly, in some cases it is – that one situation was only a brief period in someone's life, so if they continued to use after that, I'm sorry but they were making a choice.

The truth is that the majority of us use drugs because we like it; that's just how it works. Why do you think they call it a drug of choice? Many addicts will tell you, though, that the drug itself doesn't matter. Addiction isn't defined by any one substance, but by our behaviours and the thoughts and emotions that drive them.

This where I like to talk about what I call the dopamine cycle. Now, I'm not claiming to have defined this; far from it. The world is full of people far more intelligent than me, so one or more of them has undoubtedly said this long before I did. I've just never heard anyone else speaking about it, at least not while talking about addictive behaviours.

The dopamine cycle is the cycle of desire and satisfaction. It all starts when we find out that something we want exists. It doesn't matter what that is: a sexual partner, a house, a car, a better job, a pair of shoes, or a fucking bacon double cheeseburger. All we know is that it exists, and we want it more than anyone ever wanted anything.

Let's say, just as an example, that we meet someone that we're attracted to, but for whatever reason we don't make a move straight away. We go from knowing that person exists to thinking about them – in most cases obsessively, if we're being honest – to being compelled to act on our obsession and asking them out. Then finally, if all goes well, we get their number and have sex with them. That whole process of awareness, obsession, compulsion, and eventual satisfaction, is addictive behaviour in a nutshell.

We've found something that has the power to distract us or shield us from parts of ourselves and our lives that we're trying to avoid. The buzz doesn't start when we use the drug; that's just the satisfaction point, the climax, the pot of gold at the end of the rainbow. The real buzz starts when you discover there *is* a rainbow and begin chasing that pot of gold.

But then, when we eventually obtain that bag of heroin, reach that bench press, buy those shoes, or sleep with that partner, we feel dissatisfied. And that's because we were chasing the buzz of attaining those things, not the things themselves.

JUST ANOTHER ASPECT OF BEING HUMAN

Lusting after the things we want is just a natural part of being human. Our whole economy is built on people chasing shiny things that they believe will make them happy – and sometimes they do. What would life be without rewards and trinkets? Finding things, and people, both aesthetically pleasing and emotionally satisfying is part of our programming. It's only when our obsession gives us tunnel vision and blinds that our behaviours become unhealthy, to the point where we don't see or even care how damaging those behaviours are to ourselves or other people. That's when they become problematic.

There is an idea that addicts are emotionally hypersensitive, that we feel things more deeply than other people. I've already talked about the idea that negative emotions could be inherent at a cellular level, meaning that some of us could be born with what I call a negative emotional charge. If you layer that with the adverse and possibly traumatic experiences of childhood, and even adolescence, it makes sense that some of us are more emotionally sensitive than others.

Have you ever heard anyone say 'You don't know how it feels' or 'You don't know what it's like to be me'? I have, because it was me who said it. And many others have said the same, and we fucking meant it.

I'm not joking; I really meant it. When I was telling people they didn't understand, I knew that it was true, because no-one truly knows what it's like to be someone else. I believed that no-one's suffering could compare to mine, even though I had no idea how they had suffered themselves. I knew I was hurting other people, and I did care about that. But I just felt that the suffering I caused them still didn't compare to my own, so in a way it was justifiable.

And that's what changed.

As I said to my sponsor in Steps Six and Seven, I was still a young man, and I didn't want my lust or desire removed. Lust and desire are a natural part of being human, so I just wanted to learn how to self-regulate.

When I started to learn more about why I was the way I was and made the essential shift from powerless to empowerment, I stopped seeing myself as a victim. I stopped seeing life as something that had been forced on me. It was literally something I had chosen. If it wasn't, I would have followed through with my plan all those years ago and most likely have been found dead in the street.

My life, my choice, so no way to justify being a selfish bastard anymore. By the way, that is an entirely different thing from putting yourself first. It's one thing to establish healthy boundaries for your own wellbeing. But not caring how your choices impact on others because you believe you have suffered enough hardship to justify it, that's something else.

I still chase women and get obsessed about money and things, but now I know where the cut-off point is. I never leave myself with no money to pay the bills, and I wouldn't dream of manipulating another person and abusing their trust for the sake of my own interest. However, I admit I am still a masterful liar, which can be a handy survival skill to have. But as Superman always says, 'With great power comes great responsibility', and nowadays I only use my powers for good.

My life is far from perfect, but for the most part I'm happy, and that's what counts. Something I've always been honest about is that for me not using drugs is a trade-off. My life has to be better without drugs than it was with them, otherwise not using would be absolutely pointless.

We're here for a good time, not for a long time, and I've spent enough of my life feeling miserable.

USING AGAIN AFTER YOU GET CLEAN

Sometimes people ask me if I miss using, or if I'd ever use drugs again. The simple answer is, yes, of course I do. Any former drug addict that tells you they don't think about using is either in a firm state of denial or they're outright lying to you.

Yes, our using took us to some dark and disturbing places and that's why we got clean. But there's no denying we had some good times on drugs, too. Two decades is a long time for something to be so intimately involved in your life, so it wouldn't be normal if didn't think about them or even miss them from time to time.

If I don't think addiction is disease, and drugs really have nothing to do with the real cause, then why can't I use them every now and again?

Well, no-one says you can't. But there are some things that need to be taken into consideration, and the first thing to consider is why you want to use in the first place. Do you want to use because you're depressed or unhappy and think that using will somehow bring you the happiness you're struggling to find? Because it won't, I assure you.

We've all heard the phrase 'the fantasy is better than the reality', right? We humans have a tendency of romanticising things a little, and reminiscing about our drug is just like reminiscing about an ex-partner when you're lonely and you miss them. You remember the good times, how funny they were, how good the sex was, that weird thing they did with their tongue that blew your mind. And you start convincing yourself that the arguments weren't really that bad and maybe you could work things out. But you conveniently forget how miserable you, or both of you, were by the end of the relationship. Next thing you know, you've unblocked them, and you've retyped the 'Hi, how you been?' message twelve times before finally sending it.

Well, it's the same with drugs. And no-one can tell me they never had a good time at some point while they were using, because we all know that isn't true. If it hadn't made us feel good, we would never have become habitual drug users in the first place.

When I fantasise about using, I remember things like happy trips on acid or trying heroin for the first time. But the problem is that those thoughts and feelings might not stay happy.

Let's go back to triggers. Our brain remembers everything we've ever tried to forget, and all those memories are stored in our hippocampus just waiting to be woken up.

In the beginning, our romanticised view of using might make it seem like a good idea. But the memories we have stored in relation to our using aren't all happy ones. Chances are that once you put the drugs in, or more likely when they wear off, you relive all the guilt, shame, and trauma that your brain associates with using. It's like having an argument with that partner you decided to message when you were at a low point, and then you ended up regretting it.

When you have that argument, you're not just angry or upset about something they've done in that moment. You're wounded by every hurtful thing they've ever done, at the same time, because all those memories have been woken up.

For most of us, our relationship with substances is the most committed relationship we've ever been in. So, it stands to reason that those same substances that offer temporary joy have the potential to fuck us up more than any other partner ever could.

However, if you've done the right kind of emotional work, faced your demons, managed to accept yourself for who you are, found a level of personal contentment, and are generally happy about where you are in life, it doesn't have to be impossible to use drugs recreationally. What you really have to be honest about, though, is whether you want to use because you're still looking for something to shelter you from a life you feel victimised by, or because you feel that the odd joint every now and then would just be adding sprinkles to the tub of Ben & Jerry's that already is your life.

Remember, too, that being clean means different things to different people. Some people are clean from drugs but still go out drinking at the weekends. Personally, I am well aware that drinking isn't such a good idea for me. There's a strong chance alcohol would affect my ability to rationalise, and basically lead me to thinking bad ideas weren't as bad as I'd thought they would be if I was sober. I also don't think it would take a drunk me too long before thinking that cocaine would be a good idea. And before I knew it, four days would have passed, and all those old wounds would have opened back up again.

The one and only thing to indulge in is the recreational use of cannabis and THC edibles, which I've been using safely now for the past few months. Am I suggesting that you do what I do? Absolutely not. So please don't use my life choices to justify your own.

I know people will ask why I would use something like that after such a long time clean. I could tell you that it helps me manage me chronic pain conditions, and that it helps me regulate the anger management that comes with being on TRT – all of which is true. And bear in mind I took cold showers and drank my own piss for a whole month, so it's safe to say that I've given alternative therapies a fair run. But the truth is that I missed getting high every now and then… it's that simple. What can I say? I'm an honest man. And yes, I still class myself as clean. As far as I'm concerned, addiction is defined by any obsessive behaviour we're compelled to act upon because it has the power to change how we feel and shields us from things we'd rather not face.

Some readers might say I'm contradicting myself, because I've already admitted that I don't have a mind that is suited to using THC. And they'd be right; that's exactly what I said. However, I also pointed out that my mind wasn't suited to using it because sometimes THC amplifies any underlying mental or emotional health issues.

Well, back then I had an undiagnosed hormone imbalance, and I didn't even feel like a complete person, never mind know who I was. But now I have a fair idea who I am and I'm more stable than I've ever been; my mind holds no secrets for me anymore. And if cannabis wasn't there, my life would still be a happy one… and that's the difference.

I no longer feel the need for a security blanket. I just like something I enjoy, and there's nothing wrong with that as long as it's not done to excess. And my sponsor agrees, as do some medical professionals that I've discussed this with and who shall remain nameless.

PRESCRIBED HEALTH AND WELLBEING

There's a been a lot of big chat about Western medicine and pharmaceutical companies over the years, especially since Covid, and particularly on social media. But just as with the fellowships, I'm not here to prove or disprove anyone's knowledge or opinions.

However, I am a former drug addict now trained as a holistic therapist, who is now fully dependent on prescription medication that I will be taking for the rest of my life. So – and stop me if I'm wrong – I think I have enough personal experience to chip in.

I know there are some hard-core 'recovery' gurus out there who will say that if you're taking medication, you're not clean. But don't listen to them, because they're fucking dangerous.

Fair enough if you're on a methadone script, taking more medication than you should be, or taking medication that you shouldn't be taking at all. In that case, you should stop that shit as soon as possible. But don't just come off it straight away: harm reduction, remember.

Unfortunately, in my experience newcomers who are still using either get shunned, or hardly anyone speaks to them, or they are bombarded with advice that really isn't helpful. But most of them just want to know they're welcome. They have no interest in your knowledge of the big book, or how you apply the concept of Step

Eleven into your daily life. So just say hello and offer them a fucking biscuit, and stop looking for them to stroke your ego. They're feeling intimidated enough.

If you have any medical condition that requires taking medication – regardless of what that condition is – and someone who isn't a doctor tells you stop taking it, or even worse makes you feel guilty and unwelcome because you do, you have my permission to tell them to fuck right off.

I personally know two guys that stopped taking their medication because they were vulnerable and some people told them to, and it had serious consequences. One of them isn't here anymore.

Let's call the first guy Michael. Michael had schizoaffective disorder, which is basically a combination of schizophrenia and bipolar disorder. He decided it was time to get his life together, so he started going to fellowship meetings and volunteering at his local church. Then one night at a meeting, Michael was picking up a keyring to mark how many months he had been clean, and some halfwit told him that he was cheating and would never really be clean until he stopped taking his meds.

So, Michael stopped taking his antipsychotics and didn't tell anyone. At another meeting shortly after that, the group was discussing the concept of higher powers. There was a statue of the Virgin Mary holding the baby Jesus in the room, and Michael convinced himself that he was the higher power in the room. It was him the Virgin Mary was cradling. He ended up spending three months on a psychiatric ward, convinced he was the next Messiah.

The next tale is even more tragic. We'll call the next guy Patrick. Patrick didn't do meetings or fellowships; they weren't for him. He decided instead that yoga and spirituality were the path for him, and that's how we met. However, somewhere on his path someone told Patrick that microdosing DMT and psilocybin would be better for treating his schizophrenia than conventional medication. Before long Patrick was doing Ayahuasca ceremonies, and he opened doors in his mind that could never be shut. Tragically, he ended his life by jumping from a window because he was being constantly harassed by entities only he could see.

Holistic therapies and alternative treatments have their place. But using hallucinogens to treat someone's mental or emotional health issues is a complicated business. It should only be done under the guidance of someone who has some kind of authority in that particular field, not some wanker in a kaftan who spent a fortnight in Peru and came back calling themselves a shaman.

And it's not the kind of thing you can cook up in your kitchen following a step-by-step you found on Google either. If you want to do that for your own recreational use, then that's up to you, but I would advise against it for any kind of medical practice.

Am I saying that these guys weren't at least partly accountable for their own choices? Absolutely not. But they were vulnerable and susceptible to the influences of other people. So, even if you have the best intentions, think carefully about what kind of advice you give and how you choose to deliver it. You never know how it might be perceived by the minds of the people who hear it.

I've been clean for nine years, and I am completely reliant on prescription medication for my quality of life. My depression was so bad that if it wasn't for TRT I probably wouldn't be here, or there's a good chance I'd be using. While I was waiting for treatment, it was a strong consideration, and I'll be honest, I didn't just consider it once.

Then there are prescription painkillers, which are always a bone of contention when it comes to people with a history of addiction. And don't get me wrong, I'm now reliant on medication I used to abuse on a daily basis, so I can understand why there would be mixed opinions. But I went through a lot of misdiagnosis and alternative treatments before I got to where I am now. I tried different supplements, changing my diet, using essential oils, reiki, acupuncture, physiotherapy, even a full month of cold-water therapy. But none of it made any difference.

Even then, opting for medication wasn't something I just did. I had to have long conversations with my GP about the risks of someone with my background taking opiate-based medications. And my prescriptions were monitored for a full twelve months, and could only be accessed weekly by special request.

I still say that one of the only reasons my doctor agreed to prescribe me dihydrocodeine was because I told her that I didn't believe addiction was a disease, and that I was fully accountable for my choices. I've been on dihydrocodeine for over two years now, and no concerns have been raised by the GP or by me. I was being prescribed dihydrocodeine even when I was waiting on hormone treatment.

I spent four months thinking about suicide every day. And there were times when I didn't just consider using but actually decided that I was going to. Yet I still couldn't bring myself to, because in the words of He-Man: I have the power. I decide if I'm going to use – not God, not some disease, not my circumstances. Just me.

WIZARD OF OZ SYNDROME

My strength, the reason why I've managed to stay clean this long, lies in my accountability. The fact that I believe I am fully responsible for my choices. And, as we know, a belief is a powerful emotional attachment.

I don't just think that using would be my choice; I know it is. And I've faced enough challenges to know that if I really was powerless the disease would have beaten me. But it didn't. No matter how hard it got, or how easy it would have been to justify picking up that bottle or going for that bag, I didn't do it. I had switched from powerless to empowerment and become my own higher power. I had stepped in and stopped myself using when no-one else could. But it wasn't always like that.

Every journey to empowerment starts with drawing power from somewhere else. Our higher power. And it's easier to believe in someone or something we see as greater, stronger, or more intelligent than we are than it is to believe in ourselves. What we don't see is that the things that inspire us or give us hope and strength came from the words and minds of other people. Other humans that once were where we are. And if that power lies in them, it lies in us… just waiting to be unleashed.

Do you remember in the *Wizard of Oz* the Scarecrow wanted a brain, the Tin Man wanted a heart, and the Lion wanted courage. So, they all joined Dorothy Gale to ask the great and powerful Oz to give them the parts of them they thought were missing. But they then discovered that those things had been inside them all along; they had just been too caught up their own neurosis to see it. If they had ventured out on their own without Dorothy, they would have faced their own challenges and got to where they needed to be anyway. There's too many of you out there pacing the floor, scared to go outside because people won't like you or think you're weird.

Dorothy's companions were more capable than they thought they were, and so are you. You've just not learned to believe it yet. That's totally understandable, given the fact that the majority of us are conditioned to believe that we're less than we are from the day we're born. And that's even without any adverse experiences. When you throw those into the mix, it's no wonder most of us are fucked. Fucked, but far from unfixable.

Just like the Scarecrow, the Tin Man, and the Lion, all those people whose words and ideas bring you comfort and inspiration had to face trials and hardships until one day they said, 'Fuck it, I'm not putting up with this anymore.' Life took them to a place where they could either crumble and be crushed, or they could start kicking. With each trial, they survived, leaving them wondering what else they might be capable of. Then, once they had time to process their hardships and how they had survived them, they became self-actualised. They recognised their full potential, which is what makes them so awe-inspiring.

But as inspirational as these people are, they're human like you and me. And what one human can do, another can do, too. They say a journey of a thousand miles starts with a single step. For an addict, the first step is saying, 'Fuck this, I've had enough.'

THE INTIMATE RELATIONSHIP WITH THE SUBSTANCE

You hear a lot of people comparing their relationships with drugs to a toxic relationship with a narcissistic partner, and it's usually the partner's fault that they acted the way they did. Drugs made me do this; drugs made me do that. But guess what, drugs had nothing to do with it. Drugs are inanimate; they're a thing, not a they. And that thing only has the purpose or power that we assign to it – like the power to temporarily shield us from things we'd rather not feel.

Even if our quest was unintentional, that thing (whatever it is) then quickly became the centre of our universe, our reason for being. Some might say it was our original higher power, the thing that was there for us when we felt nothing or no-one else was. In most cases, our addictions are our longest-standing committed relationships, and most of us have been using longer than we have ever been with any partner.

It also knows all our secrets, our fears, our shame, and our disappointments. And that is why our emotional attachment to our addiction is so strong, and why so many people struggle to give it up.

Forget about heroin addicts for a moment and think about occasional cigarette smokers, like the guy who smokes a cigarette in secret when he's out walking the dog to help him decompress after a stressful day. That doesn't sound like anything serious, and it's not… but it is something. In that moment he's relying on a secret relationship with a substance to help make his life a little more comfortable. How do you think he'd feel if those cigarettes were taken away from him?

Your drug of choice is a thing, an inanimate object that has no purpose until it's been given one. In this case the dog walker, whether he realises it or not, has made that cigarette his emotional support. It's his emotional support cigarette. And if someone took that away, or he felt forced to give the cigarettes up against his will, perhaps because of how someone else might feel about him smoking, he might feel a little resentful. That is understandable, and I think anyone would feel resentful about that.

Now imagine that cigarette was a bag of heroin, and that bag of heroin shielded you from every bad thing you've ever felt. It took away all the bad and shameful things you'd ever done and protected you from every bad and shameful thing that had been done to you. Can you imagine how you would feel if you felt you had to give that relationship up for someone else? It's no surprise that addicts go through a grieving process when they get clean.

HOW I STARTED

Unlike some people who will tell you that they started using because they got in with the wrong crowd, or they felt pressured into it by their peers, I'll tell you straight. I may well have been introduced to substances by other people, but I kept doing it because I liked it. As an unhappy child, all my fantasies were about disappearing to another world, and drugs helped me do that. So, I kept using them.

It didn't matter who hurt me, abused me, or let me down; drugs were there to offer me protection. They were my shelter, my escape from a world that never seemed to want me there in the first place. Drugs were my friends, and I made it my mission to make as many friends as I could. It would be easy for me to say that I tried heroin without knowing what it was, which then led to a two-year dependency. But that would be a lie. I knew exactly what it was. I didn't just take it willingly, but enthusiastically.

I was living in Blackpool at the time, though how I got there is an entertaining story that I'll keep for another day.

After a bout of sleeping rough, living in squats, and eating from bins, I managed to find a permanent room in a hostel. Well, as permanent as hostel rooms get, and which turned out not to be very permanent at all.

I didn't fall in with the wrong crowd; I fell in with the right crowd – people very similar to myself. One night, after a three-day bender on ecstasy and speed, I was sitting with a girl I knew well who said she had some proper gear, if I was up for it. I knew it was one of two options: it was either crack or heroin. It turned out to be heroin.

Crack is one of the few drugs I never tried. I'd seen enough people crawling on the floor smoking carpet fluff to know that wasn't for me. And even though I'd take pretty much anything, I always did prefer downers, to be fair.

It wasn't like stereotypical heroin use, cooking up in alleyways; that came later. Instead, I was sitting in a warm room in a big comfortable chair, smoking a heroin joint. Instantly I decided it was for me. It gave me a feeling I had always been looking for and never found; it somehow made me feel complete.

Knowing what I know now about how my hormone imbalance affected my dopamine levels, this kind of makes sense. The heroin was rewiring my brain, flooding it with a chemical which my body struggled to produce naturally. But as I said, I didn't know any of that then. At that time, I just decided that heroin was for me, and I was going to keep using it.

LOVE IS BLIND

Heroin became my safe space. It was the most comfort anything in this world had ever offered me, as if God Himself was feeding my Mammy's soup directly to my soul. I fell in love with it, and as clichéd as it sounds, sometimes love really is blind. I was so in love with heroin that I didn't, or refused to, see how damaging life with her actually was.

People who knew me stopped talking to me, walking past me in the street as if they didn't know me. I suppose it wasn't really that surprising, considering my arms were covered in track marks and lumps from unsuccessful hits where I had missed the vein.

I was too busy being offended to see why they would be embarrassed to be seen with me. But no-one wants to be associated with someone who could be found in a public toilet with a shoelace round their leg and a needle hanging out of their foot.

I never overdosed when I was using heroin, but she did try to kill me once… and even that wasn't enough to stop me.

I was part of a group of three that used to go shoplifting together. I wasn't the subtle, crafty kind of shoplifter that treated it like a covert operation. No. I was the kind that walked into shops and grabbed a load of leather coats off the rail then ran down the street as fast as I could. Not the smartest way to do things, and I got caught more than once.

Somehow, though, I always managed to avoid prison – and not just for shoplifting. I've got four offensive weapon and two assault charges under my belt yet never once been convicted, and I don't fully understand the reasons myself.

Anyway, back to the story. We'd been out grafting then went to score and cook up in one of the guys' flats (I was sleeping rough at the time). We cooked up and everything was fine. As this was back in 1999, before everyone had mobile phones, we went to a pay phone to try and get more gear. But from nowhere I collapsed on the ground, spewing out bitter-tasting orange bile. Next thing I knew I'd come round naked in this guy's bed, with these two men standing over me.

My initial thought was that I'd been spiked and these two guys either had or were just about to rape me, or maybe both. So, my survival instinct kicked in, and I started swinging punches as I tried to get out the bed. But I was too weak, and it felt like my muscles had forgotten how to work. They were pinning me to the bed, and just before I lost consciousness again, I heard one of the guys say, 'He thinks we're trying to hurt him.'

The next time I came round I was still disorientated, but I was fully conscious; I was actually in the room. They had put a pair of shorts on me, and they were making soup. It was all very surreal.

It turned out that I'd had what they call a dirty hit, which is when the mix gets contaminated when you're cooking up. As a result, I had poisoned my bloodstream and almost died. These two guys had just saved my life and were now making me soup! Addicts aren't bad people, just people who have made poor choices for reasons even they probably don't understand.

However, this just shows you how strong my commitment to using heroin was. I literally poisoned my bloodstream and almost died, then I went straight back out and scored the next day. My needle fixation was so bad that I was even tattooing myself with them. I have tattoos on my knees that cover two Indian ink cannabis leaves that I did with a one ml syringe when I was eighteen. I would even inject myself with needles that had other people's blood in them. Miraculously, I never contracted any kind of blood-borne virus.

I'm sure you're wondering why someone would do that to themselves. Being a heroin addict is bad enough, but why would anyone behave so recklessly? But to fully understand that, you have to go back to those core beliefs I told you about and consider the words I used to use to describe myself: monstrous, unlovable, and less than human. In my mind I was the creature being chased through the village with pitchforks and burning torches. Back then my life meant nothing – not to me nor anyone else.

I didn't come off heroin until I came back to Glasgow. And even then, I never intended to. I actually brought gear with me, with the intention of scoring the first chance I got… and then I saw my mum. To my genuine surprise, she was happy that I was home. I've no idea why, after everything I had put her through, but it just goes to show that a mother's love truly is unconditional.

I was flooded with guilt, though. After everything I had already done, I just thought, *I can't put her through this.* I kept imagining her finding me with a needle hanging out of my arm, and what that would do to her. So, I took the heroin I had brought with me and threw it in the bin. And I never touched it again.

I'm not going to say that coming off heroin just like that was easy. And it wasn't like I was clean. I just replaced the heroin with other things like hash, valium, and alcohol, so the physical withdrawal wasn't that bad, if I even noticed it at all.

It was the emotional attachment I struggled with. I didn't give heroin up because I wanted to. I gave it up to have a relationship with my mum, and for a long time I resented her for that.

Yes, you read that correctly. I gave up heroin so that I could have a relationship with a mum who had done nothing but love and support me in her own way, and I resented her for it. This is why I always say that you should get clean *for yourself.* Doing it for someone else is a completely different type of emotional attachment that is still based around guilt and shame. I know people who even resent their own children, because the kids are the reason they can't use anymore.

People who think this way of getting clean is a choice, it's not. It's a deprivation. It's not something they want; it's something they feel they have to do. I'm not saying that getting clean for your mum or your kids is a bad thing. But if, at some point in the process, you don't realise you as a person deserve more than a life consumed with substance use, it's more than likely going to cause problems somewhere along the line.

In a sense I was lucky that my drug use took me to the place it did. Because in that moment when my life was supposed to end, I found a fragment of a thought that told me I might be worth something rather than nothing.

I didn't get clean for my brother's kids, but their love for me convinced me that I might be someone deserving of love. And that fragment of a thought is the only reason I'm here now.

GOD AND ME

No matter what way I looked at it, God was everywhere: the programme; the yoga studio; even my reiki masters said we were tapping into God's energy. So, it seemed that God was going to be part of my life whether I liked it or not. That got me curious about what God, or angels, or even demons, meant to humanity.

The more I looked, it seemed that the concept of gods originally came about by people trying to explain things we knew were important or magnificent but which we couldn't really comprehend at the time. We had gods for everything: the sun, the moon, the sky, the trees, the ocean, everything. Then, as human understanding expanded, the old gods of natural wonder were whittled down to the two that represented darkness and light and who then, along with their minions, came to represent human morality. God, with his angels. And the devil, with his demons.

It appears that as humans we've always been looking for something outside ourselves to explain or justify our behaviour, with the virtuous among us being guided by God, and the sinful being corrupted by the devil.

I'm sorry to tell you, but I just don't think that as a race we are so special that we would have two celestial entities battling it out to commandeer the rights to our eternal souls. I think people just needed a way to encourage what was essentially good behaviour and, more importantly, justify bad behaviour. And it's even acceptable to do bad things, as long it was in God's name! Countless atrocities have been carried out under God's will over the centuries.

The truth is that no-one can explain God, which is why I think the concept alone makes many people feel so uncomfortable. That's why I always find it so amusing when people say they understand God's will. The notion that a human could understand the will of a supreme being is ludicrous. Most of us can't even understand our own will, never mind the will of God.

That is probably why some people going through the programme say that God and higher powers are the same thing. But they're not. There is a clear distinction between the two. Knowing that I'm not special, I'm sure there are other people out there who faced a similar dilemma to the one I did. And being in this new world, where old gods had been reinterpreted for the modern age, makes it even more confusing for people who are just starting to wander onto their spiritual path.

When it comes to a fellowship perspective, a higher power is anything that can break the addict's cycle of thinking and offers them guidance or support. For one guy, his phone was enough, because it meant he could call someone and talk situations through. It is what they call a 'restoration to sanity' – something that helps you rationalise your thought process. But as useful as a phone call to a friend is, you can't compare that to God. And if we're following the idea that we're born with the disease of addiction and asking for knowledge of God's will and the power to carry that out, we're gonna have to understand God in a way that works for us.

Sometimes God and higher powers are the same thing. And sometimes they're not. I've even heard God being used as an anagram for Good Orderly Direction. There's nothing wrong with any of that; you do what works for you. But I had experienced too many seemingly serendipitous situations to put them down to coincidence. You can all think and believe what you want, but looking back I'm convinced that there was definitely some sort of divine intervention at play at certain points in my life.

It wasn't just that I felt some unknown force had stepped in and saved me at what could have been some pivotal life-changing moments. But I also experienced other things I couldn't explain. Signs, synchronicities, and what some people call angel numbers. It was as if something was trying to guide me or tell me I was on the right path.

Some might say that I've done too many drugs, but that day I was coming home after making peace with my dad, and hearing that song at that time… that was no accident. I believe that was my dad telling me that he'd heard me. And you already know my thoughts on the word belief. This is something I think; this is something I know.

I believe in this so strongly that I even have these so-called angel numbers tattooed on my body. But how does a guy who doesn't believe in God or angels justify his belief in divine guidance and intervention? The answer is physics. The more you look into this stuff, the more you see that science and spirituality go hand-in-hand.

My knowledge of physics is limited, I admit. I'm a writer not a scientist. But we know that energy is a constant which cannot be destroyed; it can only change form and be given a new purpose. We also know that everything in the known universe is made from the dust and particles of dead stars and planets that have been broken down and recycled since before time began.

To my mind, this would explain both cellular consciousness and what reiki practitioners call spiritual energy or intelligent energy. Nothing could exist for as long as that matter and energy had without developing some kind of consciousness. And, because that consciousness is older and more ancient than ours, it would be beyond our level of comprehension.

If the same matter and intelligent energy that makes all things – including us – has and always will exist, and those particles and the energy that brought them together has a consciousness that learns and develops over time, surely we become part of that consciousness when we die and our bodies become subject to entropy.

This is the part where you're thinking about shutting the book and putting it down because you think I've lost the plot. But hear me out. I'm about use physics to explain after-life consciousness and divine intervention, so surely that's worth sticking around for… even if it does sound like bullshit.

Let's look at how DNA was formed. There are discrepancies between scholars about when the first strands of DNA were first formed; some say it was 4.4 billion years ago. But all that matters is that at one point there wasn't DNA, and then there was. Why? Because the molecules and the energy that brings them together aren't just conscious; they have a memory. Remember our Japanese friend Dr Emoto? This explains his theory and goes deeper.

Back in the primordial swamp before creatures walked the earth, there was nothing but molecules moving around in the aftermath of the energy that created the universe, randomly colliding with one another until they learned to join together and make stuff. (I'm not a scientist, remember.) One day, after so many random collisions, they made their first nucleotide, then learned how to replicate it. Then, after fuck knows how many more hundreds of thousands – if not millions – of years, those nucleotides learned that they could spiral themselves together and create DNA.

We're not only here because of molecular and energetic consciousness, but we're also an extension of that consciousness. So, if those molecules and that energy is eternally recycled and the consciousness constantly evolving, every loved one we've ever lost exists in the cosmos somewhere. And that makes more sense than everyone living in a kingdom in the clouds no-one can see.

The religious among you will say that I'm just a nonbeliever, or maybe even a heretic. And the cynical among you will say that none of this is possible, and that drugs have given me brain damage. But have you never experienced strange coincidences that defy all explanation?

If everything is interconnected, we're all part of an eternal energetic consciousness that's continuously evolving, and our loved ones are part of that energy, it means we're connected to it emotionally. So, would it not make more sense that those loved ones existing out there in the cosmos stepped in to help and guide us when we need it most? And it wouldn't just be loved ones we knew; it would everyone we're connected to ancestrally right down the line. Those were my angels; those were my guides. And my god was the energy that held everything together.

I know someone's going to ask, 'But what about who or what created all this?' And my answer is… who gives a fuck? As I said, any sort of supreme being would be beyond our comprehension. So, instead of following someone else's doctrine, work with what you know or can figure out for yourself.

WHY I DON'T DO MEETINGS ANYMORE

When I first got clean, I did fellowship meetings every day, and I know people who still do. You can see why some people think it's a cult, but there is an energy in those rooms that no-one can fully describe. Again, some say it's the presence of God in the room, but we all know how I feel about God and energy. So, my god was definitely there.

Meetings were a big part of getting clean for me in the early days, which is why I would never say meetings were a bad idea or tell someone not to go to them... even if I don't agree with the ideology. Getting clean is a very personal thing; it's about doing what's right for you.

After a while, I felt that meetings just weren't right for me any longer. I had learned too much, and there were too many unanswered questions and bits that didn't make sense. And on my journey, I had learned about things that to me made a lot more sense, like inherent trauma, diverse childhood experiences, negative conditioning, core beliefs, and eternal cosmic energy. Certainly more sense than a God that I, and most of the people around me, struggled to believe in, or being born an addict for reasons no-one could explain.

It all comes back to the same question: was it nature or nurture? It was clear to me that it was both. Yes, inherent trauma could be classed as a form of genetic predisposition, but if so, that is something we were all born with to varying degrees, so that wasn't enough.

I soon discovered that my new opinions offended people, which I suppose is understandable. When people believe in something as strongly as fellowship people do with disease ideology, they'll dismiss it while fiercely defending the thing they believe in. But as fiercely as they defended it, a lot of them didn't practise what they preached. Again, I'm not saying it's like that everywhere, and there were people who definitely made the core teachings and values part of their daily lives. My sponsor, for example. But some of them not so much.

I found that a lot of the fellowships were quite cliquey. They tended to stick to their own little groups, and if your face didn't fit you weren't that welcome. There were lots of big egos, too. People forcing their perceived knowledge onto people, then getting a bit moody when they didn't take it on board. But the thing I really didn't like was the 'us and them' mentality which most people had adopted. There was clear distinction between addicts and what they called 'normal people', and I really didn't like that.

First of all, it just enforced the idea that people with addiction issues never could or would be 'normal people', whatever the fuck a normal person is. I've yet to meet one. And also that an addict would be an addict their whole life, regardless of how long they had been clean. That would be a fair assumption if you believed that the underlying issues which led to our using only applied to addicts. But I had already learned that wasn't true.

I knew that there were people out there who had experienced a life very similar to mine yet never drank, used a drug, or gambled in their life. They chose to cope with their challenges and trauma in a different way. Instead of trying to blank out their feelings or shut them off completely, they used them as fuel to be the best version of themselves they could be.

That 'them and us' viewpoint also implied that no-one other than an addict could understand an addict's problems. Again, if we're confining 'problems' to using drugs, then that would make sense. But they were implying that people who had never been addicts had never faced problems as big or as challenging as people who used drugs.

Personally, I just saw this as another form of justification. No-one understands us; no-one suffers like we suffer. People martyring themselves on the cross while they convince themselves that they never were and never would be like everyone else.

Again, I knew that this just wasn't the case. I openly spoke about my addiction and my problems with anyone that was willing to have the conversation or curious enough to ask. And do you know what I found? Not only could the 'normal people' identify with it, but many had also experienced the same problems as me. They'd had traumatic experiences, negative beliefs, intrusive thoughts, and some degree of obsessive-compulsive behaviour. But they just had a better handle on it.

While I had spent my whole life feeling guilty and shameful, trying to shut out all the parts of myself and my life I didn't like, these people had been strong enough to face their issues and make them part of their overall life experience. I was fascinated by the resilience they must have had. And that's what I wanted. I didn't want to be in a room ten years from now still whining about the same stuff other people handled on a daily basis.

Then there was that energy. I knew that meetings worked because the people there had a shared belief and faith in the purpose of the meeting itself. And to my mind, if I was going to the meetings without believing what everyone else believed, it made me a vampire. I would just be there soaking up energy from others while giving nothing back.

I didn't just stop going to meetings, though. I thought about it long and hard. My sponsor said that everyone went through a phase of thinking meetings were a waste of time, and that it would pass eventually. But I wasn't so sure about that.

Then, on the night that I was picking up my eighteen-month keyring, I was listening to everyone regurgitate the same things for the hundredth time, and I decided that it would be my last meeting. And I've never set foot in one since.

I'll say this again, just so we're clear. I'm not telling you *not* to go to meetings or saying they're a waste of time. Far from it. I know that meetings still help a lot of people, provide a comfortable space, and help build a support network. And I also know that there are people who attend meetings but don't agree with everything that's being said. They just take what's for them and leave the rest behind. And that's fine, too. You do you.

This is strictly how I feel about it, and I'm not asking you to agree with me or do what I do.

WE DON'T RECOVER, WE GET BETTER

I didn't start writing this book with the intention of defining the one true cause of why addicts become addicts. It was merely an attempt to help other people make sense of their journey by sharing my own, and maybe to challenge some opinions and break down some stigmas along the way. And, at my most optimistic, I hope to encourage other people who have knowledge and experiences that could help others to share their journey, too.

By now I think we can all agree that even though the true cause of why some people become addicts and some don't remains somewhat ambiguous, I have enough knowledge and experience to at least offer an educated opinion.

I expect that some people will be offended when they read this book, as they were when I spoke about my opinions at fellowships meetings.

While I don't believe that addiction can be defined as a disease, some people are very resolute in their beliefs. So resolute, in fact, that I've actually had people I might once have classed as friends take a step back from me in the street as if I was contagious. And it's all because I told them I didn't go to meetings anymore, and the reasons why. It was as if free thinking had somehow become a virus, and they might become contaminated if they stood too close to me.

Some didn't even bother to stop and talk to me, but just looked the other way, as if the very sight of me was enough to offend them.

And I'll be honest, if I have offended any of you, I'm not sorry. If you're under the impression that you have the right to go through life without being offended, or that everyone whose opinion differs from yours is automatically wrong, then you're totally deluded. Differences of opinion and challenging new ideas with old ones is part of how we grow and learn. And the fact that we pour so much money into addiction services and educating people, yet addiction is still a global epidemic, tells me that what we're doing now isn't working too well. So, any new thoughts or ideas should be welcome.

There's a big difference between explanation and justification. In my case, I wanted to understand why I was the way I was and did the things I did. I didn't want to make doing those things ok or relinquish my responsibility for doing them. But that's exactly what you're doing when you say you've got a disease that you're powerless over, or that you were in survival mode.

When you say these things, what you're really saying is, 'I did things I'm embarrassed about and not very proud of, and I do want to feel bad about it so I'm going to find a way of justifying it.'

I spread through the people who loved me like a toxic wave, affecting them in ways I'll never understand. And the most empowering thing I ever did was to take ownership of that.

No-one has to tell us what we did, because we know all too well. In the same way, no-one gets to tell us how we should feel about these issues, because we know how we feel. Taking ownership of the things we're most ashamed of is the ultimate form of control and redefines our moral compass. As we go through whatever process we choose – be that the programme, counselling, religious or spiritual practice, any combination of the three, or any other process that works for you – we learn how doing those things and seeing their impact on other people made us feel without being shielded by a substance. And the chances are there will be little chance of us behaving in the same way again.

Then there's the word recovery, which I know is the globally accepted term. Everyone that's managed to get clean or is in the process of getting clean is in recovery. I'm sorry – well, I'm not really, because this is about honesty, so people's feelings don't really come into it – when it comes to addiction the word recovery makes no sense, at least when you apply it to the individual. Don't worry, I can explain myself.

The word recovery means 'a return to a normal state', which implies that everything was going smoothly, then you hit a bump in the road that knocked you off balance, and you somehow managed to steer yourself back on course again. That would make sense if you broke your leg or caught the flu or something, but it doesn't make sense when you apply it in this situation. Again, I have discussed this with a lot of people from different backgrounds, including doctors and addiction workers, and they all agree that it makes sense, even if some of them were reluctant to admit it.

No matter how much our perspectives may vary, there are some constances we must all agree on. The first thing is that drugs don't cause addiction, and that using them to your detriment, and the detriment of others, is a symptom of a much more complex underlying problem.

Regardless of whether addiction is a disease we're born with and which no-one can really define, or it's the result of adverse experiences and disrupted development, these issues had most likely been part of our psyche before we had developed any true sense of identity. And they were one of the building blocks we built our identity on. This means that the underlying cause for our addiction was always part of who we were. So when it comes to getting clean, the word 'recovery' makes no sense.

It would make more sense if the addict got clean then relapsed, and the relapse was their 'recovery', because this was their return to their normal state.

Then are the people who say they led 'normal' lives until some tragedy befell them, and they started drinking or using drugs excessively as a coping strategy. That, in my opinion, completely dismisses the disease theory.

Our experience with substances alters us in a way that cannot be undone. So even if the person were to get clean, they couldn't go back to the person they were, because that person doesn't exist anymore. They have become a completely new version of themselves. So, that's not a return; it's a development, an evolution.

And that leads me back to the better-than-well concept. Here I am, writing a book that challenges traditional ideas about addiction, based on my own experience and with the intention of helping others. Surely that's proof enough that the better-than-well concept has some weight.

The word recovery only really applies from a social perspective. When we're in active addiction, we behave in a way that goes against the social norm, and in most cases rightly so. There's a reason we have social norms in the first place, and it's ok to test social norms and boundaries, and even break them now and again, as long as we're not hurting anyone.

The reason people are so caught up in drug addiction isn't the drug use itself, it's the behaviours that come with it. Most people couldn't care less if addicts used drugs without bothering anyone, unless it's someone they love or care about. But when you go out and commit criminal acts or start sliding down lampposts in front of their kids, people tend to have a problem – and again, rightly so.

This is where the word recovery comes into play. When addicts get clean, they're seen to return, or 'recover', to a level of behaviour that society deems to be safe or normal.

But for the addict themselves, it goes much deeper than that. When someone gets clean, they go through a process of change that no-one could possibly understand unless they'd been through it themselves.

When I got clean, I had to break down the whole belief system my identity was built on, as I slowly came to realise that I wasn't the unlovable monster I truly saw myself to be. I had to heal my childhood self and make peace with the darker parts of me and the things I had done. I had to come to terms with the fact that I hadn't just been welcome in a world I'd felt excluded by, but that world was full of people that were just as messed up as me but who just managed their problems in a less destructive way than I did.

I didn't 'return' anywhere; I became a completely new version of who I was, and I'll be fucked if I'm going to have someone downgrade my journey by telling me I'm in 'recovery'. I haven't recovered anything. This is all completely new ground.

My name is Tony and I'm not an addict. I'm a human being with deep-rooted emotional problems that I had to learn how to manage. And if I can, so can you. Anyone can if they want it badly enough and are ready to put the work in.

I see my addiction as nothing more than a form of obsessive-compulsive disorder, and the clue is in the description. We obsess over substances and are compelled to act on our obsession.

With drugs I found something powerful to protect me from all the parts of myself I was trying to avoid. But now that I've accepted myself and my life for what it is, I no longer need protecting.

Life isn't steady; it isn't stable. It's a rollercoaster of emotional experiences, and sometimes we just have to learn to ride it out. But things only continue to hurt us if we hold onto them.

You are not defined by your past, so do what you have to do to let that shit go, learn to heal yourself, and go and be the version of you the world has never fucking seen.

And if reading this book has helped you somewhere along the way, then I've done more than I could ever hope for.

ABOUT THE AUTHOR

After two decades of slowly crumbling under the weight of my addiction, I was forced to make a choice. Open my wrists to save myself from the world, and save the world from me. Or continue on an uncertain path without knowing where I would lead. As we can see, I'm still here.

Since then, I have spent the last nine years trying to understand both the man I was and recognising the full potential of who I could become. In that time, I have studied both psychology and sociology. I have also taken part in yogic, shamanic, and witchcraft practices. I am a trained counsellor, holistic therapist, and mindfulness facilitator.

During my work in the care system, I have used my own unique approach to help others battle their own demons. Now I am sharing what I have learned with you, in the humble hope I can help other people find a version of themselves that they feel comfortable with.

Tony Donachy

www.ingramcontent.com/pod-product-compliance
Lightning Source LLC
Chambersburg PA
CBHW030437010526
44118CB00011B/683